A LETTER FROM PETER MUNK

Since we started the Munk Debates, my wife Melanie and I have been deeply gratified at how quickly they have captured the public's imagination. From the time of our first event in May 2008, we have been able to host what I believe are some of the most exciting public policy debates in Canada and internationally. Global in focus, the Munk Debates have tackled a range of issues such as humanitarian intervention, the effectiveness of foreign aid, the threat of global warming, religion's impact on geopolitics, the rise of China, and the decline of Europe. These compelling topics have served as the intellectual and ethical grist for some of the world's most important thinkers and doers from Henry Kissinger to Tony Blair to Christopher Hitchens to Paul Krugman to Lord Peter Mandelson to Fareed Zakaria.

Let me say a few words about why we started this program and why we believe so strongly that the Munk Debates should originate out of Toronto, Canada. As a Canadian who wasn't born in this country, a country that has accepted me with open arms and provided me with endless opportunities, I believe strongly that Canada must be a vital participant in world affairs. That was the primary reason that Melanie and I helped found the Munk

School of Global Affairs at the University of Toronto, my alma mater. It was the same thinking that led my Aurea Foundation to launch the Munk Debates. We wanted to create a forum that attracts the best minds and debaters to address some of the most important international issues of our time, and make these debates available to the widest possible audience. And we wanted Toronto to be at the centre of this international dialogue to affirm Canada's growing role as a world economic, intellectual, and moral leader.

Melanie and I are very pleased that the Munk Debates are making significant strides toward fulfilling the mission and spirit of our philanthropy. The issues raised at the debates have not only fostered public awareness, they have helped all of us become more involved and therefore less intimidated by the concept of globalization. It's so easy to be inward looking. It's so easy to be xenophobic. It's so easy to be nationalistic. It is hard to go into the unknown. Globalization, to many people, is an abstract concept at best. These debates are meant to encourage further engagement with the forces, good and bad, of globalization and the ancillary geopolitical issues that define our era in human history. The purpose of this debate series is to help people feel more familiar with our fast-changing world, and more comfortable participating in the global dialogue about the issues and events that will shape our collective future. It is essential today that we equip ourselves, and especially young people, with the skills and inclination to become vital and engaged participants in global affairs.

I don't need to tell you that there are many, many burning issues. Whether you talk about global warming or the plight of extreme poverty or genocide or our shaky global financial order, there are many critical issues that matter to many people. And it seems to me, and to the Aurea Foundation board members, that the quality of the public dialogue on these critical issues diminishes in direct proportion to the importance and the number of these issues clamouring for our attention. By trying to highlight the most important issues at crucial moments in the global conversation, these debates not only profile the ideas and solutions of some of our brightest and most concerned global citizens, but crystallize public passion and knowledge, helping to tackle some global challenges confronting humankind. Just as important, they seek to make Canada the forum, where Canadians and the international community can observe world-class thinkers engage each other on the big issues of the day.

I learned in life — and I'm sure many of you will share this view — that challenges bring out the best in us. I hope you'll also agree that the participants in these debates not only challenge each other, but they challenge each of us to think clearly and logically about important problems facing the world.

Peter Munk
Founder, the Aurea Foundation
Toronto, Ontario

SHOULD WE TAX THE RICH MORE?

This edition published in 2013 by
House of Anansi Press Inc.
110 Spadina Avenue, Suite 801
Toronto, ON, M5V 2K4
Tel. 416-363-4343
Fax 416-363-1017
www.houseofanansi.com

Distributed in Canada by
HarperCollins Canada Ltd.
1995 Markham Road
Scarborough, ON, M1B 5M8
Toll free tel. 1-800-387-0117

Distributed in the United States by
Publishers Group West
1700 Fourth Street
Berkeley, CA 94710
Toll free tel. 1-800-788-3123

Permission is gratefully acknowledged to reprint "Figure 1" on p. 16 to Michael I. Norton
and Dan Ariely, *Perspective on Psychological Science* 6 no. 1 (2011): 9–12 © 2011 Michael I.
Norton and Dan Ariely. Reprinted by Permission of Sage Publications.

House of Anansi Press is committed to protecting our natural environment.
As part of our efforts, the interior of this book is printed on paper that contains 100%
post-consumer recycled fibres, is acid-free, and is processed chlorine-free.

17 16 15 14 13   1 2 3 4 5

Library and Archives Canada Cataloguing in Publication

Should we tax the rich more?
Pro: Paul Krugman and George Papandreou. Con: Newt Gingrich and Arthur Laffer.

(Munk debates)
Debate held May 30, 2013, Toronto, Ontario,

Issued in print and electronic formats.
ISBN: 978-1-77089-421-1 (pbk.). ISBN: 978-1-77089-422-8 (html).

Income distribution. 2. Rich people — Taxation. 3. Taxation.
4. Fiscal policy. 5. Equality.
I. Gingrich, Newt, panelist II. Krugman, Paul R., panelist
III. Laffer, Arthur B., panelist IV. Papandreou, Giõrgos A., panelist
V. Series: Munk debates

HC79.I5S56 2013 339.2   c2013-902782-3   c2013-902783-1

Library of Congress Control Number: 2013938673

Cover design: Alysia Shewchuk
Text design and typesetting: Colleen Wormald
Transcription: Rondi Adamson

Canada Council   Conseil des Arts
for the Arts   du Canada

ONTARIO ARTS COUNCIL
CONSEIL DES ARTS DE L'ONTARIO

*We acknowledge for their financial support of our publishing program
the Canada Council for the Arts, the Ontario Arts Council, and the Government of Canada
through the Canada Book Fund.*

Printed and bound in Canada

MIX
Paper from
responsible sources
FSC® C004071
FSC
www.fsc.org

ANCIENT FOREST ™
FRIENDLY

SHOULD WE TAX THE RICH MORE?

KRUGMAN AND PAPANDREOU VS. GINGRICH AND LAFFER

THE MUNK DEBATE ON ECONOMIC INEQUALITY

Edited by Rudyard Griffiths

ANANSI

CONTENTS

CONTENTS

INTRODUCTION BY RUDYARD GRIFFITHS

Great debates occur when you get the right speakers, talking about the right issues, at the right time. On all these counts our debate on taxing the rich more than surpassed expectations. Arguing for the motion "Be it resolved, tax the rich more" was the formidable team of Paul Krugman and George Papandreou. Rightly celebrated as one of the pre-eminent public intellectuals of our time, Paul Krugman received the 2008 Nobel Prize in Economics for his groundbreaking work on international trade and economic geography. He is also a columnist with the *New York Times* and author of the paper's renowned blog on economics and politics, *The Conscience of a Liberal.* In addition to teaching economics and international relations at Princeton University, Professor Krugman has written a series of bestselling popular books on the 2008 financial crisis and its aftereffects, including *End This Depression Now!, The Return of Depression Economics and the Crisis of 2008*, and *The Great Unraveling*.

Complementing Paul Krugman's in-depth theoretical knowledge of economics with hard-won, real-world experience was his partner George Papandreou, the former prime minister of Greece. George Papandreou's practical knowledge of government policy was formed over a lifetime of engagement in politics, culminating as prime minister at the height of the European and Greek financial crises. He has also served as the president of Socialist International — the worldwide organization of social democratic, socialist, and labour parties — since 2006. Educated in Canada and the United States, George Papandreou was named by *Foreign Policy* magazine as one of the "Top 100 Global Thinkers" for having made "the best of Greece's worst year."

And one superstar team of debaters deserves another. In Newt Gingrich and Arthur Laffer we were fortunate to have recruited a powerhouse duo who could make the case *against* taxing the rich more *and* match the in-depth knowledge and experience of Krugman and Papandreou.

Newt Gingrich is a former Speaker of the U.S. House of Representatives and twice a candidate for the Republican Party nomination for president. Called "the indispensable leader" by the *Washington Times*, he is best known as the architect of the anti-tax Contract with America, which saw the Republican Party capture a majority of seats in the U.S. House of Representatives for the first time in four decades. Working with then president Bill Clinton, Speaker Gingrich passed two back-to-back balanced budgets in late 1990s — the first such occurrence in over forty years. Never the typical politician, Newt Gingrich is the author of twenty-four books, including fourteen fiction and non-fiction *New York Times* bestsellers. He is a regular commentator on public policy issues and currently co-hosts the CNN politics and current affairs show *Crossfire.*

Given how much of the debate over whether to tax the rich more revolves around historical precedents — both pro and con — who better to have at the debate arguing alongside Newt Gingrich than the person most often lauded as the "father" of supply-side economics, Arthur Laffer? One of the key economic advisers to President Ronald Reagan, Arthur Laffer was singled out by *Time* magazine as one of the century's "greatest minds" for popularizing the Laffer Curve, the claim that lower tax rates can stimulate government revenues by increasing economic output. He is the co-author of *The End of Prosperity: How Higher Taxes Will Doom the Economy — If We Let It Happen*, and the chairman of Laffer Associates.

As important as experienced and knowledgeable debaters are to creating a battle of the wits and brainpower, great debates are separated from good debates by the issues that animate them and their importance to public conversation as a whole.

This much is certain: from Europe to North America, "tax the rich more" has become a clarion call for governments of most advanced economies — and for good reason. The combined one-two punch of the financial crisis — slow to no economic growth matched by rising public debts and persistent deficits — has thrown into question the long-term sustainability of the entitlement programs that many Europeans and North Americans take for granted. Layer over these anxieties the perception that poor and middle-class incomes are stagnating while the wealthiest in society enjoy spectacular income gains, and a healthy dose of wealth redistribution through higher taxes on the rich seems not only prudent public policy but a basic issue of fairness.

Given concern about growing economic inequality, Arthur Laffer and Newt Gingrich clearly faced an uphill battle (58 percent of the 3,000 attendees voted in favour of the motion prior to the debate). But those who would have forecast, from the event's outset, a landslide victory for Paul Krugman and George Papandreou missed a key ingredient of the Munk Debates: their unpredictability. It is entirely in the debaters' hands as to how skilfully they present their arguments and counter their opponents over the course of the two-hour contest.

In this far-ranging and hotly contested debate, both teams presented a range of detailed arguments to back up their advocacy *for* or *against* higher taxes on the wealthy. For the two debaters on the "con" side, exhibit A for pushing back vigorously on higher taxes for the wealthy was Arthur Laffer's eponymous curve. As was explained to the audience, at one end of the Laffer Curve you have a tax rate of zero, which produces no tax revenue. At the other end you have a tax rate of 100 percent, which also produces no tax revenue, given that essentially all meaningful economic activity would grind to a halt if all wealth creation was expropriated by government. Common sense, therefore, tells us that somewhere between a tax rate of zero and 100 percent is a level of taxation that produces the greatest amount of tax revenue (the top of the curve). The key point that Arthur Laffer hammered home in the debate is that tax cuts can generate less of a loss in tax revenue than we would assume by using simple arithmetic (for example, a 50 percent reduction in the tax rate halves tax revenues). This is supposedly because of the stimulating effects of tax cuts: they encourage people to increase their economic output, thereby producing more taxable activity.

The much-cited example of the Laffer Curve at work is the period in the 1980s when Arthur Laffer was an economic adviser to President Ronald Reagan. As he and Newt Gingrich repeatedly reminded their opponents, President Reagan slashed the top marginal tax rate from 70 percent to 30 percent, and the federal government's revenues almost doubled between 1980 and 1990.

For disciples of Reaganomics, such as Arthur Laffer and Newt Gingrich, higher tax rates have the opposite effect than what is intended. Increased tax rates cause revenues to grow more slowly than simple arithmetic would suggest due to the disincentives they create for work, risking capital, production, and so forth. Both believe this dynamic is strongest among the ultra-wealthy, who are more sensitive to tax increases, especially when enacted on top of such a high starting tax burden. Instead of paying more to government in tax revenue, the ultra-wealthy either work the tax system with their accountants and lawyers or cut back on investment and capital expenditures, which, in turn, hurts economic output.

For more than a few audience members, Arthur Laffer's description of the elegant interplay of tax rates, government revenues, and economic activity led them to rethink whether significantly higher taxes on the rich produce a windfall in government revenues and surging economic growth.

Newt Gingrich's contribution to the debate was to evoke the moral impetus of the anti-tax movement, which currently stands centre stage in the U.S. political scene. He posited that while issues of fairness and social equity are not unimportant in advanced societies, they are not at the core of the debate over taxation. For Newt Gingrich, "the power to tax is the power to coerce" is the only maxim that ultimately matters when it comes to discussing taxation. In his view, enacting significantly higher taxes on the wealthy sends a clear and destructive message both within and about a society. Gingrich bluntly articulated that when government starts singling out the wealthy for special tax levies, what it is really saying is "get successful enough, and we're going to rip you off." During the debate he evoked the likes of Bill Gates of Microsoft and investment guru Warren Buffett as examples of individuals whose companies have created incredible wealth, not only for themselves but also for others. Newt Gingrich argued that increasing taxes on people mainly because they are rich creates powerful disincentives for the next generation of Bill Gates and Warren Buffetts, who will not want to risk their sweat equity and capital to create wealth. While others have derided this type of trickle-down economics, it clearly struck a nerve with audience members concerned about the lacklustre productivity growth and high unemployment, which have been signature marks of a frustratingly slow economic recovery.

But are these kinds of arguments against taxing the rich convincing enough to stave off concern over rising economic inequality in advanced societies and the pervasive sense that the wealthy, not the middle class or the poor, seem to disproportionately benefit from the economic policies that followed the 2008 financial crisis? Over the course of this hard-fought debate, Paul Krugman and George Papandreou advanced a number of powerful appeals for why fairness and practicality demanded enacting significantly higher taxes on the wealthy.

Right from the start of the debate, Paul Krugman wasted no time in taking on the Laffer Curve and the overall view that higher taxes will impede economic growth, though he did agree with Arthur Laffer that there is a top marginal tax rate that optimizes government revenues without damaging economic output. Citing his own work and that of other economists, Paul Krugman expressed his belief that the tax rate on the rich should be anywhere from 70 to 80 percent or at least significantly higher than the 40 percent average for OECD countries; the economic benefits of a higher top tax rate are too important to ignore, said this Nobel Laureate. Paul Krugman vehemently disagreed with Newt Gingrich's opinion that high rates create societal disincentives for work and investment, leading to slower economic growth or worse. As a counter-example to Arthur Laffer's roaring 1980s of low taxes and higher government revenue, Paul Krugman pointed to the presidency of Bill Clinton. In his first term, President Clinton raised taxes and instead of cutting economic growth, roughly 250,000 new jobs were created every month during the first two years of his administration. For Paul Krugman, the entire Clinton presidency is a refutation of trickle-down economics: "the effective tax rate on the top one percent of Americans was higher than it was in any year under the Bush I administration or the Bush II administration, and the U.S. economy experienced an epic boom despite those high tax rates."

The audience was clearly attracted to the optimism of Paul Krugman's central argument: raise taxes on the rich, use the proceeds to invest in high-quality public services for the disadvantaged and middle class, and see your consumer-led economy grow by leaps and bounds. And here George Papandreou skilfully built on his partner's principal contention by recounting his own country's journey into financial ruin and why social solidarity, as much as economics, demands that the wealthy pay more taxes. Specifically, George Papandreou warned the audience that in Greece, wealth had come to mean far more than just economic power. The country's political and legal systems, as well as its tax code, allowed elites to thwart any meaningful redistribution of their wealth. The result was spiralling deficits, ballooning public debt, and the absence of working institutions that could allow his government to collect — let alone raise — taxes to meet its financial obligations. As George Papandreou bluntly stated during the debate, "instead of a trickle-down economy, we had a trickle-out economy."

For a socialist statesman such as George Papandreou, taxation — especially of the rich — is a basic prerequisite for social equality. Simply put, the future health of society — measured in terms of educational outcomes, personal well-being, life expectancy, and similar such indicators — trumps whatever stimulating effects the toleration of more, rather than less, economic inequality has on prosperity, productivity, and innovation. He argued that "there is a democratic demand in our society to have a more equal society, to have a more equal and just economy." To no small degree the divergent philosophies of George Papandreou and Newt Gingrich mirror the different ideological approaches that North America and Europe have taken in recent decades toward how best to balance economic growth and social development. For the audience, having these starkly contrasting views on the same stage at the same time made for some of the debate's liveliest and most thought-provoking exchanges.

Finally, great debates are defined not only by the weightiness of the issues they seek to illuminate; the state and play of the larger public conversation is key to the drama and intensity debates generate. From the Occupy Wall

Street movement to government policy and legislation to the larger questions about how we create economic prosperity in the fast-changing global economy, the debate over taxing the rich more will be with us for the foreseeable future. All of us associated with the Munk Debates hope that this book helps move forward the conversation of this important public policy issue. Debate, like few other modes of discourse, gives us the range and, at times, the extremes of a particular argument or issue. Our task is to open our minds to this play of ideas, come to our own informed conclusion, and then act on it for the betterment of each other and ourselves.

Rudyard Griffiths
Moderator and Organizer, The Munk Debates
Toronto, Ontario

Should We Tax the Rich More?

Pro: Paul Krugman and George Papandreou
Con: Newt Gingrich and Arthur Laffer

May 30, 2013
Toronto, Ontario

THE MUNK DEBATE ON ECONOMIC INEQUALITY

RUDYARD GRIFFITHS: Ladies and gentlemen, welcome to the Munk Debate on economic inequality. My name is Rudyard Griffiths. I have the pleasure of organizing this debate series and the privilege of once again acting as your moderator.

I want to begin tonight by welcoming you, the over 3,000 people who've filled Roy Thomson Hall to capacity for yet another sold-out Munk Debate. All of us associated with this series really appreciate your enthusiasm for the simple idea to which this series is dedicated — that having more and better debates on the big issues facing the world and Canada can only be good for us as global citizens. Hello also to the national television audience watching this debate on the Business News Network (BNN) and CPAC across Canada and on C-SPAN across the continental United States. And hello to you, our online audience watching live right now in the thousands; it's terrific to have you as virtual participants in tonight's proceedings.

Now, we are mere moments from getting our contest underway and our four big thinkers out on stage to debate the burning question: Should we tax the rich more? But first I hope you will join me in a warm round of applause for our hosts of this evening, the Aurea Foundation and its co-founders, Peter and Melanie Munk. Tonight would not be possible without their generosity and foresight. Bravo.

Let's start getting our debaters on the stage and our debate underway. First, please welcome the former prime minister of Greece, the current president of Socialist International, and one of *Foreign Policy* magazine's "Top 100 Global Thinkers," George Papandreou. His fellow debater on the "pro" team is a Nobel Laureate in economics, a tenacious columnist and blogger with the *New York Times*, and the scourge of billionaires everywhere — ladies and gentlemen, Paul Krugman.

One formidable team of debaters deserves another, and we have them for you now. Please welcome first the intellectual "father" of Reaganomics, the author of the famous Laffer Curve, an economist who proudly proclaims that he has never seen a tax cut he didn't like, Dr. Arthur Laffer. Joining Dr. Laffer on the "con" side of this debate is none other than former U.S. Speaker of the House of Representatives, a recent candidate for the Republican presidential nomination, and one of the most influential politicians of his generation — the Honourable Newt Gingrich.

Two final orders of business before we get underway with our opening statements: first I'm going to ask our projector operator to show the debate countdown clock. Those of you who have been to Munk Debates before will remember that we have a clock, and when it hits its final moments, we want you to join me in a loud round of applause for our debaters during their opening and closing statements. That is going to keep our debate on time and our debaters on their toes.

Finally, it's time for a pivotal moment, gentlemen. We're going to see how this audience voted on tonight's resolution, "Be it resolved: tax the rich more," as they came into this room. Let's have the results of the first audience vote now. There you have it: 58 percent in favour, 28 percent opposed, and 14 percent are undecided. Let's drill down a little bit deeper with our second question because we want to see just how big that potential swing vote is in this audience. We asked, depending on what you hear here tonight during the debate, are you open to changing your vote? Let's have that number, please. Wow — 79 percent of you say yes; only 21 percent say no. So, this debate is still very much in play.

Now it's time for our opening statements. As is convention, the side arguing in favour of the motion will speak first, and Paul Krugman has offered to kick off his team. Paul, you're up.

PAUL KRUGMAN: Good evening. Thank you for the invitation and thank you all for being here. I'm delighted to be in this lovely city, which, among other things, appears to have a much more interesting mayor [Rob Ford] than any city I've ever known. But that's not what we are here to talk about. We're here to talk about taxing the rich.

There are some big philosophical and social issues involved here and I believe that my colleague, George Papandreou, is going to address those more specifically. I'm actually going to keep my part fairly mundane. I want to talk about three cut-and-dried issues. The first is should we be thinking about raising anybody's taxes? The second is can we, in fact, raise significant sums by taxing the rich more heavily? And third, should we really fear the economic consequences if we do raise taxes on the rich?

To answer the first question, we are living in a time, certainly in the United States, but also here in Canada, in which we are constantly being told that there are good things, humane things, that we would surely like to do, but that we can't afford because we are short of money. Right now the debate that I've been tracking a lot in the United States involves food stamps. Food stamps have been a crucial lifeline to a lot of people during this difficult economic time, but the House Republicans just voted for major cuts to the program, about $2 billion a year. So, would taxing the rich make any difference for this kind of issue?

It turns out that if you look at the top one percent of taxpayers in the United States in 2011, they had a combined income of about $1.4 trillion, not counting capital gains. So, if you could raise one-seventh of one percent of their income in additional revenue that would obviate the need for these food stamp cuts we are being told we need to make. Ideally I want more revenue than that because there are a lot of other programs I want to defend, but this number suggests to me that there is a lot of money at the top, enough for it to make a significant difference in allowing us to have a better society than the one we're heading for in our current trajectory.

Can you actually collect a lot more money from the top? Will raising taxes just drive the rich to take their income underground, causing them to hide it? We have a lot of evidence on that. For the United States, our top marginal tax rate has, over the generations, ranged from as low as 28 percent to as high as 91 percent. We have a lot of variation, and a lot of economists who are taking on careful statistical work to analyze it. And it *is* true that our marginal tax rates do cause reported income to decline some, but not much.

We actually have very good estimates of how high the top rate has to be to put us on the wrong side of the Laffer Curve, and those estimates are at least 70 percent, probably 80 percent or more. From where we are now, we are just not in a region where we have to worry about taxing so heavily that we could actually end up losing revenue. We can collect a lot more revenue and put it to good use if we're willing to raise tax rates at the top.

And finally, what about tax rates and the economy? Will raising tax rates on the wealthy really have disastrous economic consequences? That's what you always hear, and the classic example came some time ago, twenty years to be exact. In 1993, then newly elected President Clinton raised the top tax rates, and there were many predictions that this would have terrible effects on the economy.

A fellow by the name of Newt Gingrich made a famous prediction: "The tax increase will kill jobs and lead to a recession and the recession will force people out of work and into unemployment and actually increase the deficit." You knew this was coming right, Newt? Now, I actually know what your answer is going to be because this has happened to you before. You're going to say that it's because all the good stuff happened to the economy after Republicans took over Congress and started cutting taxes, but that's not accurate. First of all, because during those first two years of the Clinton administration, the U.S. economy added 6.7 million jobs — 278,000 a month — before you guys moved in. And secondly, those later tax cuts were small compared with the initial tax increase. Every year that Clinton was in office, according to the Congressional Budget Office, the effective tax rate on the top one percent of Americans was higher than it was in any year under the Bush I administration or the Bush II administration, and the U.S. economy experienced an epic boom despite those high tax rates. Interestingly, we now have a top rate for a few people that is back to Clinton-year levels. I didn't hear so many predictions of disaster this time because I think people have figured out it doesn't really happen that way.

And, by the way, the post–World War II generation had much higher tax rates. The United States had tax rates that would be considered inconceivable now, and that didn't stop those twenty-five years from being the best period of economic growth and the best period of middle-class rise in living standards that we've ever had in our history.

So, should we raise taxes on the rich? Yes, for various reasons, but above all because we could use the money. Can we actually raise more money that way? Yes, of course we can. The evidence is clear. Should we be afraid that it would hurt the economy? No, we shouldn't. So let's do it.

RUDYARD GRIFFITHS: Very well done, Professor Krugman, with twenty-five seconds to spare. There's nothing better than when you find those quotes to turn against your opponents! We like that. Speaker Gingrich, you're up next.

NEWT GINGRICH: Let me say first of all, I'd like to thank Peter Munk for his involvement in creating a civic institution like this one. And I do want to commend the 21 percent of you who honestly said they don't care what the four of us say tonight; that you are not going to change your minds. This may mean that Canadian audiences are somewhat more candid than American audiences, who would have said yes but not meant it.

I want to approach this from a very different angle than Paul. First of all, the debate is not about raising

9

the tax rate. We've had 70 percent tax rates, we've had 90 percent tax rates, but if you were rich enough and had really good attorneys and CPAs [Certified Public Accountants], you never paid those taxes. We just had a presidential campaign in which Mr. Krugman's candidate ran against my party's candidate partially on the grounds that my party's candidate had an effective tax rate of 14 percent, which was all legal.

It was a lot like what just happened to the secretary of commerce, who turned out to have misstated her taxes by $80 million. But that wasn't a big mistake because she is worth about $1.2 billion. So, compared to you and me, it would be like us filing $300 wrong. The fact is, really rich people don't earn incomes, they get money. That's why Bill Gates has lots of money. And that's why he doesn't care what the tax rate is — he's not going to pay it.

So, I want to make three quick cases. Let me start first with morality, then move on to practicality, and then close with a question of focus. As a matter of morality, I love the way it's phrased: "Raise taxes on the rich." Why? What do we mean by "rich?" You live in a neighbourhood; you drive a certain kind of car; the person next to you drives a better car. They happen to like cars; you happen to like something else. But since they drive a better car, should we tax them more? And, if so, why?

You have another friend who happens to work at two jobs, and therefore they have a slightly higher income because they actually earned it. So, should we raise their taxes? Why? Remember, this is not about charity and contributions and morality. The power to tax is the power to destroy. The power to tax is the power to coerce. Are we really prepared to say, "If you're successful enough, we should rip you off? You owe it to us. How dare you be so successful?" If that's our strategy, then the right answer is not to go out and create some fancy tax rate that their lawyers will get around.

We know roughly how much Bill Gates and Warren Buffett are worth. Why should they have more than a billion dollars net worth? Right there, we can get $100 billion this year — just out of two people. Why should they be allowed to be that successful? The American answer has always been, "Well, you know, Windows is a big deal; Microsoft is a big deal. It improved the lives of lots of people." The fact that it made one particular person successful is the way we encourage another generation to say, "I'd like to go and invent Microsoft."

Now you could send a different signal: "Why waste your time? If you get successful enough, we're going to rip you off." So, I would argue that just on a moral level — in wartime, in a crisis, you could say to people, "We need everything we can get." But as a strategy, to say to people in general, "If you're successful, we're going to punish you," is a bad thing morally.

Second, as a practicality, I want to send a signal to people: "Come to America, be an entrepreneur, create jobs, create wealth, create new ideas. We will reward and honour you because we believe that pulls people ahead." The Chinese have followed this strategy and created lots of billionaires. They have moved 600 million people into the middle class in a generation. So, I think this strategy works if the price is dramatic, radical economic growth, and moving 600 million people into middle-class status. I think that is good, not bad. My goal is to raise the bottom, not to lower the top. And my goal is to find a way to help everybody. So, our number one focus ought to be on jobs and on creating opportunities for everybody and on solving the problem of the permanent poor by figuring out what has kept them permanently poor.

Lastly, I think whether or not to tax the rich more is the wrong focus for politics. Big government today is a failing, centralized, bureaucratic institution, yet the private sector has been dramatically improving. Look at the hand-held device that almost all of you are carrying tonight. Look at all the breakthroughs we're making in lowering costs and increasing capabilities. And then look at the inadequacy of government.

And I'll just close with one example: there's an organization called Udacity, which was created by the head of the Google driverless car system. The goal of Udacity is to lower the cost of college education by 90 percent by improving access to learning. Now, there is a world out there we could dramatically improve, but it's not a function of taxation, it's a function of breaking out of the boxes we've been put in. And I think focusing on how to improve people's lives would be a lot better goal than trying to figure out how to punish people for being successful.

RUDYARD GRIFFITHS: I can see those Republican primary debates have kept you sharp and on your toes, Speaker Gingrich. That was a great opening statement. Up next, George Papandreou, speaking for the "pro" team.

GEORGE PAPANDREOU: First of all, let me thank you because when I was only a teenager, Canada was very hospitable to my family, who were in exile because of a dictatorship in Greece. Thank you, Canada.

It's an honour to be here with these speakers because I think we are talking about a very important issue: inequality. And everybody knows that there is soaring inequality, even more than in the 1920s, and this inequality has undermined basic principles of fairness, justice, and trust in our societies. So, I am in favour of this proposition because I believe that our democracies need to ensure fairness and a just society.

I admit this is a value I cherish. But beyond the moral imperative that I feel is important, I'd like to relate a personal experience to you. When I became prime minister, I inherited a huge deficit, made by a previous conservative government, so I had to raise taxes. But actually, my main task was to revamp the tax system because there were loopholes, there was a lack of transparency, and a lot of tax evasion. Worst of all, the Greek people — who were already paying for this massive debt — also had to pay back our financial lenders, who were supported by a global financial system that aided tax evasion through tax havens and offshore companies. So, instead of a trickle-down economy, we had a trickle-out economy.

It's estimated that about a third of total global assets are beyond the reach of effective taxation. Thirty-two trillion dollars were offshore in 2010 and were not taxed. Revenues are lost this way. So much is lost that we could have achieved the millennium goals that the UN set for poverty and climate change five times over. So, when I say inequitable tax, I also believe in strong, reformed global governance, which must include transparency, closing loopholes, and effective financial regulation around the world.

A second point: tax revenues. Of course, this is a democratic decision for each country. I believe in progressive taxation because it is the bloodline of a social contract or, if you like, a basic bargain in our societies. The conservative argument is that we need a race to the bottom because of global competition. They say we should emulate the emerging economies with lower taxes, lower wages, lower benefits, lower environmental standards, less education, and less of a safety net for health and pensioners. They are essentially proposing to undermine the basic bargain that holds our society together.

Is there another way? Gordon Brown, former prime minister of the U.K., said we need to overhaul our economies and infrastructure, invest in high-tech equipment, and promote high-quality education; that doing so will give us the skills to innovate and create future iPhones and BlackBerrys. And that is what he says is going to be the firepower to deal with the emerging economies of China and India. Otherwise, he says, we will have a decline of the West.

But thirdly, business does benefit from this basic bargain — countries like Sweden, Finland, and Germany have high taxes, but their economies are highly competitive because they have invested in human capital.

Finally, the argument that we often hear is that if you have high taxes, there will be tax avoidance because the lobbies will push for change. As a former prime minister, I have seen a huge concentration of wealth in our societies and around the globe, which has undermined democratic politics. We are captive to these interests, and that means governance — good governance — does not exist because we are not ultimately focused on the public good. And that, I believe, is a new threat to our democracies.

When the idea of democracy was conceived in Ancient Greece, it was intended to disrupt the concentration of power. And today, the concentration of power is undermining our justice system, our politics, and our public good. That's directly opposed to the intention of a democracy.

I'd like to end with a slide; it shows that there is a democratic demand for economic equality. Look at the first bar — that is what the real income distribution is in the United States; the second bar shows what people believe the income distribution is; and the third is what people — across the board despite politics — want the distribution to be.

So, there is an overwhelming demand in our society to have a more equal and just economy and society. And I think there is a reason for that. If you look at the more equal societies around the world, all the indexes show

PERCENT WEALTH OWNED

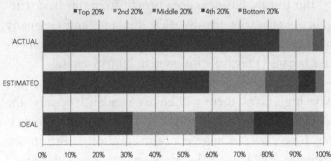

FIGURE 1: BUILDING A BETTER AMERICA — ONE WEALTH QUINTILE AT A TIME

that they are top on almost everything: whether it's life expectancy, health, or jobs. They are the most efficient and most humane societies, which is why we need equality.

RUDYARD GRIFFITHS: Well done, and that's probably in your third or fourth language, so, impressive indeed. Up next, Dr. Laffer, you're going to conclude our opening statements.

ARTHUR LAFFER: Thank you very much. By the way, Paul, that was a great one on the mayor.

I had a little experience just before coming over here tonight. I was in the health club at the hotel. It's a beautiful city here and I thought I'd exercise a bit. As some of you can tell, I'm not much of an exercise freak. So, I was down in the health club working on the machines. I didn't even break into a sweat or anything. But this gorgeous lady walks into the health club — I mean, just *absolutely* beautiful. And I happened to be on the machine next to the manager of the health club, so I tapped him on the shoulder and said, "Excuse me, but do you by any chance have a machine that would attract someone like that to someone like me?" And the man said, "Yes, I do, in fact," and he walked me over to the BMO [Bank of Montreal] ATM.

Let me just say I believe the aspirations that all three of you have mentioned are correct. The question is what happens in the real world? I'm going to tell you that if you raise tax rates on the rich, you will *not* get the money you expect and you will probably lose money completely. Look at the U.S. tax codes. We put in the progressive income tax in 1913, and at that time the highest marginal income tax rate was 7 percent. By 1919, we had raised that rate to 77 percent. We had a depression going into World War I. And after World War I, in 1920, we had a campaign between the Democratic candidates Cox and Roosevelt, who wanted to keep Woodrow Wilson's tax rates high, and the Republican candidates Harding and Coolidge, who wanted to drop the tax rates. The Republicans won and cut the highest tax rate in America from 77 percent to 25 percent, and this period became known as the Roaring Twenties. Employment and production soared during this time; tax revenues from the highest one percent of income earners, as a share of GDP, not just in dollars, went way, way up. Then we had the 1929 Smoot-Hawley tariff, the largest tax increase on traded products; we raised the highest marginal income tax rate during the Depression from 25 percent to 83 percent. There was an economic depression during this period, and tax revenues from the highest one percent of income earners declined as a share of GDP.

Then you go to the post–World War II period with Truman's cotton tax rates — again a boom. And again, tax rates on the rich went up as a share of GDP. Look at the period of Jack Kennedy — he cut the highest tax rate from 91 percent to 70 percent, and as a result, we had the go-go '60s, a beautiful period of expansion. Tax revenues from the highest one percent of income earners went way, way up as a share of GDP.

Then we had the period I like to call "The Four Stooges" — Johnson, Nixon, Ford, and Carter — the largest assembly of bipartisan ignorance probably to ever exist in the United States. They raised taxes throughout the period and, of course, revenues as a share of GDP declined from the top one percent; the economy was in shambles.

Then we had Ronald Reagan and Bill Clinton, two administrations that cut taxes dramatically. From 1980 to 2007, the revenues from the top one percent of income earners went from 1.6 percent of GDP to 3.1 percent of GDP — a huge surge in revenues from the highest income earners. We cut taxes from everything that crawled, jumped, swam, flew, and dug holes — it didn't matter what it was — we cut their taxes. Revenues from the bottom 95 percent actually went down during this period.

You know, when you look at the evidence, it is very clear — raise tax rates and you don't get money. These people, as George Papandreou says, can avoid taxes. They have the ways and the means. They can hire lawyers, accountants, income specialists, and lobbyists. They can change the location of their income, the timing of their income, the composition of their income, the volume of their income — they aren't going to pay more tax. So if you raise rates, they are going to get around it. They can do it fairly easily.

What we really have to do is lower rates and broaden the tax base to collect money. You can all see what happened in Britain recently. When [David] Cameron became prime minister the first thing he did was raise the highest tax rate on income earners from 40 percent to 50 percent. And what happened? A double-dip recession with revenues going way down.

You can even look at what is happening here in Canada. During the recent period, tax rates on corporations were at 15 percent. You've restrained yourselves on stimulus spending and your economy did far better than the U.S. did during the last six or seven years of the most recent recession. Your unemployment rate at the beginning of this period was way higher than in the United States, but it didn't go up nearly as much as it did in the United States over the years. In fact, the Canadian unemployment rate is now lower than the Americans'. If you look at Canadian debt levels today, you've done a much better job than the United States. What we need to do today is not fool around with this ad hoc approach to raising tax rates. We need total tax reform. We need to tax all income across the board. We need to tax unrealized capital gains and all these things that are tax-exempt — the 501(c)(3), all these gifts that are supposedly charitable — tax them one flat rate across the board.

Raising tax rates and wishing it would do some good will only delay us from fundamental tax reform, which we need right now. Thank you.

RUDYARD GRIFFITHS: Dr. Laffer, with that elegant opening argument, I think you've put paid to the notion that economics is a dismal science. Well done. It's now time, gentlemen, for us to dig into the table that you've set for this debate. I think we're going to have plenty of time to talk about the economics, but I want us to start by talking about the politics of this debate because I think it is on the minds of many people in this audience.

Speaker Gingrich, let me begin with you. It was recently reported that the richest 400 people in America command more wealth than 150 million of their fellow citizens, of your fellow citizens. So, outside of any economic consideration, why would you be opposed to taxing the rich as a tool to help prevent America from backsliding into the Gilded Age or a plutocracy?

NEWT GINGRICH: Well, I'm going to start with putting the question back to you, in a sense: Under what right can the state step in and say to somebody, "We have now decided that you are doing too well and we are now going to punish you for that?"

20

PAUL KRUGMAN: I get a little . . . what's the appropriate debate-friendly word?

RUDYARD GRIFFITHS: Ornery.

PAUL KRUGMAN: I was looking for something more like "pissed off," but anyway. If you start saying, "Why do you want to punish the rich?" I consider that basically a confession of intellectual bankruptcy because nobody on my side ever says that that's what it is about. It is never about punishing the rich. I don't hate the rich. Actually, some of my best friends . . .

NEWT GINGRICH: You are one.

PAUL KRUGMAN: I'm high enough to be hurt by the policies I advocate. I don't have anything against the rich; I just want some of their money to pay for essential programs. And I think it's worth saying.

I thought it was interesting that Newt Gingrich mentioned that some people have suggested a way to drastically cut the cost of a college education. I hope they can. But, you know, there's a funny thing. We used to have a way that middle- and working-class kids in the United States could get a college education: it was by going to excellent state universities that were heavily subsidized. That option is largely gone now because the subsidies are gone, and state university tuition has gone way up as a result. And so we need more money, and one way to get more money is by taxing the rich. It's not going to solve all of our problems, but it will solve some of them.

And I just want to say that it's sad that some are arguing we should base our tax policy on the belief that the United States — a modern, twenty-first-century nation with all the institutions of democratic governance — is completely incapable of policing tax evasion; that it is hopeless; that we are basically a Third-World country. We are Venezuela!

RUDYARD GRIFFITHS: It's a good point.

NEWT GINGRICH: No, wait a second. Look, Paul has made two totally different arguments. The first argument is that we need all this money because government is inefficient and prices keep rising dramatically. Take the example of education. What's happened to the salaries of faculty members? What's happened to the number of bureaucratic administrators? Why has education become so expensive? Nobody who is for government wants to talk about the necessary rethinking of how we spend money. And so I start with the question: Before you tell me we need to raise taxes, are you really prepared to defend the current government?

But I find the second thing you said very chilling. We are in the early stages of an IRS scandal in which IRS agents, who have enormous power, are saying things like, "What prayer were they saying at the meeting? That eighty-three-year-old woman who held Friday morning coffee sessions, what exactly was she doing?" You both may be comfortable with a government so powerful that it can guarantee that nobody will escape taxation, but I am frightened by a government that powerful.

GEORGE PAPANDREOU: First of all, I am not saying that I am in favour of government or in favour of markets. I grew up in Greece when we had a dictatorship, so I didn't like the state then because it was a very authoritarian state. We need government to be democratically accountable to our citizens. The concentration of wealth today means that the government is not serving the public good; it is serving special interests. And that is the problem — the democratic problem.

Newt, I don't think you're against government. I think you're in favour of government. But you are in favour of government for very specific interests, for big business. I'm in favour of government that will serve the people and the public good. And I'm not against the markets; I just want to make sure that the markets also serve basic principles.

ARTHUR LAFFER: Yes, but Mr. Prime Minister, no one disagrees with you on that.

GEORGE PAPANDREOU: Good.

ARTHUR LAFFER: Everyone wants government to serve the people. The question is do we want government to raise tax rates? The answer to that is I don't think it serves the people. We need to focus on serving the people better, and we can do that through tax reform. Through tax reform we can create prosperity and we can generate revenue. We need a broad-based tax without all these loopholes, all these deductions, exemptions and exclusions, and with lower rates. This is the whole principle behind Simpson-Bowles. We also did this in the '86 Tax Act. In this case, we lowered the highest income-tax rate in the United States from 50 percent to 28 percent. We raised the lowest rate from 12.5 to 15 percent. We cut the number of tax brackets from 14 to 4. We dropped the corporate rate from 46 percent to 34 percent. And the vote in the Senate? Ninety-seven to three in favour, including Alan Cranston, Mister Left-Wefty, including my neighbour and great friend Al Gore, including Bill Bradley, Teddy Kennedy, Joe Biden, Chris Dodd, and Howard Metzenbaum; they all voted for it because they knew it was the right thing to do to generate growth and to get revenues for government and reduce the need for spending.

PAUL KRUGMAN: I have looked at some careful economic studies of the '86 Tax Reform Act, which, by the way, was widely admired. I do believe that equalizing the tax rate on capital gains, on different forms of income, is the right way to go . . .

ARTHUR LAFFER: Yes it is.

PAUL KRUGMAN: However, there have been many studies that have attempted to identify the effect of that tax reform on the rate of U.S. productivity growth and U.S. potential output, and they haven't found a damn thing. It's just not visible.

ARTHUR LAFFER: [Martin] Feldstein's work on this has shown the effects of the '86 Tax Act very clearly by following the same cohorts using IRS data. If you look at all of these —

RUDYARD GRIFFITHS: Gentlemen, let's —

PAUL KRUGMAN: You know something? We need to step outside and throw spreadsheets at each other.

RUDYARD GRIFFITHS: Good point! Let's pull up from the minutiae, which are important, to look at the big picture. Speaker Gingrich, why do you believe that fundamentally you are going to get the growth to lift all boats through a policy of not taxing the rich, and why do you think Paul Krugman and George Papandreou are wrong?

NEWT GINGRICH: Well, let me first go back to a point that the prime minister made, because it is important to understand the kind of gap we're talking about here. Four hundred families have a lot of power, fine. You want to actually raise their taxes enough to take away that power? Now you're back to what I said earlier. You want to take enough money away from Bill Gates so that he doesn't have power? That's like from $53 billion to $1 billion, and even at a billion, I think billionaires have a lot of power. So you get down to a question: What are we talking about here? What are we trying to accomplish in terms of the signals we send about the kind of society we live in?

Now let me come to your specific question. The primary reason the poorest people in America are trapped in poverty is because government fails them; the government schools fail them; the neighbourhoods fail them; the employment market fails them. Look at Chicago with over five hundred people killed in 2012 — the public safety system certainly failed them. I would like to see civic discourse focus on asking questions like how radically do we have to reform the experience of poor Americans to allow them to break out and give them a chance to genuinely climb? I'm more interested in the next thousand people rising from poverty than I am in trying to go out and find somebody whose pocket I can reach into to take money from. And I would argue that at $4 trillion a year, the problem with the U.S. government is not absence of money, it's absence of competence.

GEORGE PAPANDREOU: I'll come back to that.

Look at Europe — there are incompetent governments, but also very good governments that are accountable, democratic, and transparent. The point of transparent government is not simply to weaken the concentration of power, which I do believe affects politics. I have been a prime minister and I know how media and politics can be controlled when you have such a huge, amazing concentration of power. What I want, however, is to empower our citizens through taxation because I see our citizens today are not free. They are very dependent. They are very dependent because there is huge unemployment around the world, in the developed world, and they're not getting the basic needs and services they want.

In countries where you have higher taxes and where government is efficient, you get a good education system, a good health care system, a sense of public cohesion, and a highly competitive economy. Why? Because you have invested in the human capabilities to allow these people to be independent — they can feel free to be innovative and look forward. So, I believe that —

ARTHUR LAFFER: But that's not saying you should raise tax rates. We all agree with everything you've said. The question is how do you get the money? You won't get what you want by raising tax rates.

To address your example of Sweden — they've been one of the world's biggest tax cutters. Have you seen their performance recently? It's amazing what has happened in Sweden. The best way to achieve your dreams and your goals of a truly democratic government is by lowering tax rates and broadening the tax base so that everyone pays their fair share, which will get you the requisite revenues to create prosperity.

GEORGE PAPANDREOU: Sweden is not in favour of a flat tax — they have a very progressive tax rate. And recently the inequality in Sweden — the rise in inequality in the last few months — has created riots in some of the suburbs. So, I think we need to understand that a truly cohesive society is one that is much more equal.

RUDYARD GRIFFITHS: Paul Krugman.

PAUL KRUGMAN: One thing — actually no, two things. Art Laffer has given us a history of U.S. tax rates and all I can say is that none of it is true. America has become — among the advanced countries — the land of least opportunity. It has become the country where people who start at the bottom have the least chance of making their way up. We have people who are more trapped in poverty, more trapped in poverty from generation to generation, more trapped in the bottom quintile, than in any other advanced country. And a lot of that is not just because government is failing or is doing its job badly; it's because government is not doing its job.

Here's one example: many children don't have adequate nutrition. It is really hard to work your way up to get a good education and work your way up to the middle class if you're hungry all the time, and a lot of kids in America are hungry all the time. It's really hard to work your way up if you're sick all the time and not treated, and a lot of children in America don't have adequate health care. And the reason they're not given those things is not because of general philosophical principles, or at least that is not the way it is sold. It's sold as we don't have the money: "You can't raise any more money by taxing the rich because, if you do that, it'll destroy our economy." So don't tell me that it is not the real issue because it is certainly an important part of our story.

RUDYARD GRIFFITHS: That's a good point to transition on. Let's go to the first of our video interventions. We did this last time with some success, so we're going to experiment with it again. The contributor is former U.S. Treasury secretary, former economic adviser to President Barack Obama. Let's listen to Larry Summers.

LAWRENCE SUMMERS: Yes, we should tax the rich more in the United States. In the United States we have growing pressures on the public sector, a rising population over sixty-five who are nearing or past retirement, and rising relative prices of things that governments buy — education and health care. The relative price of health care and a television set has changed by a factor of a hundred over the last generation, and the public sector buys health care.

We also, of course, have rising debt burdens. That's going to put pressure on the public sector. Some of it needs to be met by cutting wasteful spending, but there isn't that much wasteful spending to cut, so revenues are going to have to increase. Where should that come from? On grounds of fairness, it should come from the wealthy. On grounds of the major changes that have taken place over the last two decades, it should come from the wealthy, whose share of the top one percent has gone from less than 10 percent a generation ago to more than 20 percent.

And it should come from the wealthy because they are the ones who have been able to escape and avoid the most taxation over the years through a range of inappropriate tax loopholes and tax expenditures.

RUDYARD GRIFFITHS: Speaker Gingrich, I'm going to come to you first on this because this is a key part of this debate, especially here in Canada. With an aging society and a shrinking workforce, there is a sense that we are all going to have to pay more to cope with the demographic challenges that much of the West faces. So, in a sense, why hasn't history given the nod to this side of the debate and said, "You know, you're right. Everyone is going to pay more, including the rich?"

NEWT GINGRICH: Let me take two examples. First of all, let's look at Dr. Krugman's appeal to children who don't get adequate food, and so forth, in a country that has a women's, infants', and children's program, has food stamps, has prenatal care, and has a program in schools specifically designed to help children eat properly. Maybe he's commenting on the ineffectiveness of government to reach every poor child who needs adequate nutrition despite spending billions of dollars. And, if so, the problem is not that we're not spending a lot of money to ensure that poor children have nutrition, it's with government. So that's important to set in place.

But Larry Summers said one thing there that I thought was amazing, that I don't think Larry understood he said. He said that the difference in television price versus health care has changed by a factor of a hundred, meaning televisions are a hundred times less expensive today relative to health care than they were, say, in 1960 or 1950. He doesn't then stop and say, "Gee, why is it in the private sector we are able to produce, for example, cellphones at declining costs with rising capabilities and we can't get the same kind of breakthroughs in government-controlled areas?"

If we have the courage to do it, we are on the edge of a breakthrough in how we think of government as a whole; I'll give you a specific example. I'm a conservative and therefore I'm supposed to be pro-defence, which I am. But I always tell people, "I'm a hawk, but I'm a cheap hawk." I think you could take 20 percent out of the defence budget and have a more agile, more effective, better defence department — we just need to modernize. And so, before I raise taxes to pay for a bloated, inefficient, oligarchical defence system that is really running behind the world, running behind reality because it can't keep up with change, I would rather fundamentally overhaul the Pentagon. Then you come talk to me about taxes.

But don't tell me I have to tolerate every bureaucratic incompetence, including some of the things — the failures — that Paul Krugman has mentioned. Why shouldn't we overhaul the entire system of helping poor children if, in fact, what he is saying is true? Because we spend billions of dollars in multiple bureaucracies and, according to Dr. Krugman, we are failing to get the job done.

PAUL KRUGMAN: One correction — you said earlier that you knew "the candidate I favoured" in the last presidential election. As a *New York Times* columnist, I am not allowed to do endorsements, so you have no idea who I favoured in last year's election.

RUDYARD GRIFFITHS: It probably wasn't Mitt Romney.

NEWT GINGRICH: Paul, I may have no proof, but I have an idea.

RUDYARD GRIFFITHS: This is true.

PAUL KRUGMAN: To go back to the issue of helping the poor. We actually spend a fair bit on poverty-related concerns, but what we spend on helping the poor is something well under half the share of GDP that Canada spends, so don't talk about how vastly generous we are. We are not. We are the least generous of all the advanced countries when it comes to helping the poor.

And as it happens, food stamps are very much on the firing line. We are talking about cuts in the current agricultural bill. Paul Ryan [U.S. Budget Committee chairman] has called for savage cuts in the food stamp program and, as it happens, that is a program that the government does very, very well. Bureaucracy is minimal, the spending goes to the right people. But there just isn't enough funding. It is not enough to ensure that everybody who needs nutritional assistance receives it; the sums are too small. Health care? We've done a good job. Medicaid is actually a surprisingly efficient program. Health care happens to be one of those areas where government consistently is more efficient than the private sector. But again, it is not enough. If you're going to use electronics as your standard of comparison why not ask: "Why can't we make haircuts as cheap as we manage to make smartphones?" That's a really, really bad argument.

RUDYARD GRIFFITHS: Let me bring George Papandreou into this. Mr. Papandreou, if cynicism about government exists anywhere, it is probably in your home country of Greece right now. So why, in the context of this debate, are these gentlemen wrong in terms of people saying, "Look, these systems aren't working; they don't need more money, they need overhaul reform." Do they need financial pressure, the fear of the reduction of funds, in order to reform themselves?

GEORGE PAPANDREOU: My mandate during my campaign was to change government and make it more transparent. And I had to deal with big pharmaceutical lobbies that were milking the pension system with very costly medical treatments. And, if I'm not mistaken, in the American discussions about Medicare and the changes in the health care system, Congress did not pass a bill to allow central procurement, which is the bargaining power of the central government — the federal government — vis-à-vis the pharmaceutical companies. Why? Because pharmaceutical companies can get better prices if they bargain with each hospital individually. Now that to me is bureaucratic inefficiency. But it's bureaucratic inefficiency, not because of socialism, but because of the power big business wields over government. And that is what I was fighting in Greece. We had crony capitalism; we had to change. Pharmaceutical companies created so much waste that I had to bring in electronic prescriptions to cut out about 30 percent of it; thankfully, I was successful.

I would add one other thing. Business needs a functioning state, and a functioning state that provides basic needs, such as good education. In many European countries, businesses are able to fire people very easily, but the welfare state comes in and says, "I'm going to train you — retrain you — and I'm going to get you back into the job market and you're going to be even better then." And you know what that does? That is a boon for business, and that is why those businesses are competitive. So I don't want to punish business. I just want to make sure that money is used in the right way. We definitely need higher taxes if we want to create the conditions for our citizens to be free and capable people.

ARTHUR LAFFER: I agree with all that, but this is not the point. The question asks whether or not we should raise tax rates on the rich. The best form of welfare, as John F. Kennedy said, is still a good, high-paying job. It's far better to get the people off welfare with jobs. People don't become prosperous with handouts. They become prosperous with jobs. Benjamin Hooks said —

GEORGE PAPANDREOU: I'm not talking about handouts —

ARTHUR LAFFER: I agree with you about making every-thing efficient and making it better, and no one wants to let those people who are down and out not get what we can afford as a society — we all want that. What we want to do is create prosperity. Benjamin Hooks put it so well. He was head of the NAACP [National Association for the Advancement of Colored People]. He said that blacks are hired last and fired first, and the only way blacks are ever going to get jobs and keep them is if there are so many jobs around they've got to be hired. Prosperity is the answer; it's the answer to all the things; it's the answer to tax revenues. If we can provide dra-matically more services than Ethiopia, it's because we are more prosperous than they are.

Don't kill the prosperity. If you tax people who work and you pay people who don't work — do I need to say the next sentence to you? Come on! Help me on this!

RUDYARD GRIFFITHS: Art, you're eloquent; you've had your time. But I want to get Paul Krugman in on this, and then I want to move on to another question.

PAUL KRUGMAN: I'm disappointed in the sort of cosmic nature of these arguments, as if we're talking about destroying the fundamental nature of America, as if the kinds of tax changes that we might be contemplating are things that would have stopped Steve Jobs and [Steve Wozniak] from trying to invent a computer in their garage. We're not talking about that. We're not talking about punitive taxation; we're just talking about somewhat more, to provide somewhat more benefits. And I think that by phrasing it as if it's all or nothing — as if we should not even attempt progressive taxation, not attempt to provide benefits financed in part by that progressive taxation, that those taxation levels will destroy everything — is wrong.

What we do know — and I think this is where the Scandinavian stories do come in — is that here you have societies that collect 40 percent or 50 percent of GDP in taxes and they function. They function very, very well. That tells you right away that the notion that taxes are, in themselves, extremely destructive can't be right. There is a lot of evidence that suggests we could focus those taxes on the rich — that we could raise a significant amount of money by having a progressive tax system. We wouldn't be able to concentrate all the taxes on the rich, but we certainly could focus some of them. We shouldn't be asking are you for a free society or not? I mean —

NEWT GINGRICH: The question is rather global. It didn't say tax the rich more; it didn't say tax the rich less or a little more or a lot more. The prime minister suggested we should tax the rich enough to redistribute power away from the four hundred families. That's a lot of tax. But let me ask you about a specific example: Would you regard [French president François] Hollande's 75 percent tax on the wealthy as too much or too little? I mean, it is clearly leading a lot of wealthy Frenchmen to decide they love Luxembourg. Is that within the Krugman worldview?

PAUL KRUGMAN: Actually, I don't think France can do it because France is one piece of Europe, and it is too easy to move to Luxembourg. I think if the European Union as a whole did it, it would be workable. I think if the United States did it, it would be workable. My former colleague and Nobel Laureate Peter Diamond has crunched the numbers as best he can, and his estimate is that the optimal top tax rate is, as it turns out, 73 percent.

ARTHUR LAFFER: Not optimal, the highest revenue.

PAUL KRUGMAN: And we used to have that, by the way. We had tax rates in that range all throughout that great generation of postwar growth. So, am I actually suggesting that the United States try to match Hollande's tax rate? No, because I know it doesn't have a chance of happening. But do I think that a move in that direction is okay? Yes. Do I think that what Hollande is doing is crazy? No.

NEWT GINGRICH: So, one more question.

RUDYARD GRIFFITHS: Quickly because I want to be conscious of our time.

NEWT GINGRICH: I'm sorry, but I think this is a useful dialogue. If you're going to go to a 73 percent rate, if you could do it by a magic wand, would it be the 1950s-style 73 percent rate, with large enough loopholes that nobody paid it, or would it actually be a cleaned-out system so you're actually going to get 73 percent?

PAUL KRUGMAN: I think if it is at 73 percent, you are going to have to have some differentiation for capital income, but not nearly as much. And, by the way, if you actually look at what the effective rates of taxation were on the top one percent back in the '50s, they were high — they were over 50 percent, but maybe not 73 percent.

RUDYARD GRIFFITHS: Gentlemen, in our remaining minutes here, I want to internationalize this debate a bit because it is not just about Canada and the United States. This is a conversation that is happening around the world. And to do that, I want to go to our final video contribution for tonight. It's from a big thinker from Asia. Kishore Mahbubani is the dean of the Lee Kuan Yew School of Public Policy in Singapore. We caught up with him via satellite recently. Let's listen to his intervention.

KISHORE MAHBUBANI: Thank you, Rudyard. About twenty years ago, a group of Chinese economists came to New Delhi to meet a group of Indian economists, including the current deputy chief economic planner, Montek Singh Ahluwalia. They explained to the Indian economists what reforms they were planning to undertake. When they finished, Montek Singh said to them, with some trepidation, "Do you realize that if you carry out these reforms in China, there will be more inequality?" The Chinese economists smiled broadly and said to Montek, "We certainly hope so!" And that's exactly what happened.

As China progressed, it produced the largest number of new billionaires in the world. But at the same time, China also carried out the largest poverty-reduction program in human history, lifting over 600 million people out of absolute poverty. It also produced a very large new middle class. So you can see that as long as the rising inequality also benefited the majority of people, the Chinese and Asians accepted it.

RUDYARD GRIFFITHS: Good point and an important one in this debate. Let's have George Papandreou weigh in on this first. We'd kill ourselves right now to be able to lift people out of poverty and get 6, 7, 8 percent GDP growth, wouldn't we? So why is the Chinese model wrong?

GEORGE PAPANDREOU: Absolutely. But I would disagree with him. I don't think this growth is predicated on inequality. I think it's because the Chinese government invested heavily in industries. And yes, this inequality brought people out of poverty, but there are a host of other problems facing China that threaten to hinder this growth.

First of all, the Chinese realize that they don't have a pension and a welfare system. They have an aging population. The one-child-per-family actually worked.

So there is going to be a big burden on the younger generation to care for the older generation, which will be problematic. They also have to cater to the needs of a new working class who are asking for higher wages. Employees who work for manufacturing companies — assembling iPhones for Apple as one example — and those who work in other industries are asking for better working conditions. Thirdly, China has a major environmental problem. Soon Beijing will not be environmentally viable. The government realizes that it needs more money to create a better society.

I don't think it's inequality that has helped them; inequality has actually undermined a more cohesive society. I believe China will slowly move toward a more equal society by investing in a social safety net that will help the Chinese people.

RUDYARD GRIFFITHS: Paul wants in on this, but I'm going to go to Speaker Gingrich first. You mentioned China in your opening statements. George Papandreou thinks the model, if not broken, is in serious trouble. Can you comment on this?

NEWT GINGRICH: I think China's problems are a by-product of its own success. For example, China now has so many cars that they have to deal with massive air pollution. China now has so many people working that they have all sorts of transportation issues. China now has so many people producing goods and services that they have to return to a very rudimentary environmental policy.

One of the great moments in human history is that unlike sixty years ago, the Chinese have generated enough wealth that they can actually deal with the next generation of problems. In 1930, the poor Chinese would have been dealing with starvation and slavery; they would have had no hope and been at a level of poverty that is almost unimaginable. So, I think the Chinese will tell you that yes, they've got big problems, but they're a big country, and they're going to have some big solutions.

GEORGE PAPANDREOU: So obviously Newt is in favour of central planning. Right, Newt? In China?

NEWT GINGRICH: I'll talk about that in my closing statement.

RUDYARD GRIFFITHS: So the more billionaires the better? China allows billionaires to thrive; it allows inequality; it doesn't go after the rich hard — not in the way that you would want, Paul?

PAUL KRUGMAN: I've spent a lot of time on these issues. Latin American countries have looked at these ideas a lot. Twenty years ago there was widespread acceptance of the so-called Washington Consensus, which said, don't worry about inequality; focus on liberalizing your markets and you'll get those wonderful Asian takeoffs. And a bunch of Latin American countries, including Mexico, more or less did that. And they liberalized and some good things happened, but there were no takeoffs.

Growth just didn't happen. It must have been really disappointing.

And after a long time we looked and tried to figure out what it was that the Asians actually had that the Latin Americans did not have. And it turns out that the Asian countries had really well-educated populations; they had really good infrastructure. And it turns out that just having policies that let inequality flourish without providing those other things does not, in fact, produce growth.

And in the last ten years or so, countries like Mexico have actually started to tackle inequality seriously and it's working: inequality is coming down; poverty is falling fast — through government action, I might add not through the magic of the marketplace. It looks like this is actually starting to improve their growth prospects as well because of better nutrition and better education. So the actual lesson is not "China has inequality and China succeeds." We need to look at some comparisons, and it turns out that just letting the rich run wild is not enough.

RUDYARD GRIFFITHS: Back to you, Art Laffer — the rich running wild! I like it.

ARTHUR LAFFER: Paul, you're so right. The rich shouldn't just run wild. But we're talking about raising tax rates in a tragically flawed system that has all sorts of loopholes and where all forms of income aren't taxed equally. The rich are gouging the system, but not because tax rates are too low. It's because you haven't defined income properly; you haven't put it in the right context. It is a tragedy what is happening.

Look at what happened in China. They did three things: cut taxes, created a hard currency, and opened markets — the three pillars of supply-side economics. And what we've seen is massive growth and prosperity from 1979 on. Yes, Newt is totally right. These problems Paul is talking about are those associated with prosperity, not poverty. China prior to the implementation of supply-side economics was educated, but they were in really bad shape. They now have a different set of options.

RUDYARD GRIFFITHS: Gentlemen, it's time now for closing statements. You get to settle scores with each other in your remaining three minutes each. We're going to do our closing statements in the opposite order of the opening statements. So, Art Laffer, you're up first.

ARTHUR LAFFER: I'm going to start with one example of a man who has been trying to raise tax rates on the rich for a long time. His name is Warren "Buffay." He's of French origin from Omaha, Nebraska — I'm talking about Warren Buffett, by the way. He has been saying, "Me and my friends have got to have higher tax rates; we all think we should pay more."

Let me take you through Warren Buffett. He wrote a letter to the *New York Times*, explaining that he paid a little less than $7 million in taxes, but that was 17.4 percent of his income and he had the lowest tax rate of any of the people in his office — that it was half the tax rate of his secretary. Now, I'm a math whiz, so I took his $7 million and his 17.4 percent tax rate and I divided it to get his income, which I discovered was a little bit less than $40 million. Now, that's a large, large level of income.

But let me tell you what also happened to Warren Buffett in 2010, when he reported $40 million in income. His wealth, in unrealized capital gains, which is not taxed, rose by $10 billion. His gifts to the Bill and Melinda Gates Foundation, which are tax-free, were $1.6 billion. I didn't find out how much he gave to his sons' and his daughters' tax-exempt foundations. As an economist, at least to me, income is what you spend, what you give away, and the increase in your wealth. So, to me, his income in 2010 was $12 billion. And he paid $7 million in taxes, which is six one-hundredths of one percent of his income. That is not fair. But all the tax rates he wanted to raise were the ones he doesn't have to pay.

We shouldn't raise tax rates as they currently stand. We should change the tax code and lower tax rates. Now, I did Jerry Brown of California's flat tax when he ran for president in 1992 and we had two flat-rate taxes, one on business net sales and one on personal unadjusted gross income. No other federal taxes — none. And if you had just the 12 percent tax on Warren Buffett, it would be $1.44 billion. That is what I consider fair. Thank you.

RUDYARD GRIFFITHS: Fighting words. You're up next, George Papandreou.

GEORGE PAPANDREOU: Thank you. I've never asked, and I don't think Paul is asking, to punish the rich. We're saying that as a global society, we have created so much wealth — in the United States, in China, in Europe — that is highly unequally distributed. All we're saying is we could use some of that amazing wealth that is in the hands of a few thousand people around the world. It could go a long way.

We have major issues we have to deal with going forward, like climate change and unemployment. In my country, there is a youth unemployment rate of close to 60 percent. Now is that a sustainable society? We need to give those young people training, hope, and job prospects. So, in relation to the rich, we're talking about them giving back a small portion of their wealth to their governments to make our societies more just, better, and more efficient, and to help us prepare for major challenges the younger generations will face.

In all studies we have seen that more equal societies perform better in all categories: life expectancy, math and literacy rates, infant mortality rates, teenage birth rates, obesity rates, and even happiness levels. Even the rich live longer in equal societies, so we're not punishing them. They will benefit.

Finally, I want to tell you about a personal experience I had. I had the curse of being exiled, but the blessing of coming to Canada. I came from a country that was not only a dictatorship, but where there was no real social contract of any kind. There was no bargain between the government and its citizens, or between the different classes. And I believe that if we don't have a just society, we will have class warfare. I don't want this, I'm advocating for the complete opposite — a cohesive society — and I found it here in Canada. Despite all its difficulties, Canada is a country that welcomes refugees, migrants, and is able to integrate them because it respects, helps, and invests in them. Canada invested in my family and me and in people generally, which brings me to my point.

Today we need to use some of the wealth that exists to invest in the human capacity of our society and of our citizens, and in doing so we will not only have a more efficient and competitive economy, we will have a much better economy, a much better society, and a much better life. Thank you.

RUDYARD GRIFFITHS: Speaker Gingrich, your final words.

NEWT GINGRICH: First of all, let me start by addressing the almost 60 percent youth unemployment rate in Greece, which is a tragedy. Let me ask: What is the underlying lesson we can learn about a system that has failed so decisively that 60 percent of its young people don't have a job?

I'll give you two examples. I was inspired by the last message from Singapore. I had a chance to spend time with Lee Kuan Yew, a senior minister who has helped develop modern Singapore. I asked him, "What was the key to why you were so successful?" And he said, "I was a graduate student in Great Britain during the Labour government right after World War II. And I watched everything they did to create a socialist society. And when I finally got to be prime minister of Singapore, every time I'd encounter a problem I'd say to myself, what would the Labour government have done? And I would then do the exact opposite. I wanted work ethic to be important. I wanted people to save. I wanted the rule of law."

Now let's look at this whole question. There are two key things to mention: practicality — what works — and whether you favour freedom or the state, which is a permanent tension in every society.

What works? There is a bridge in Nanjing, China, which has two giant statues: a black cat and a white cat, and its symbolism is derived from a famous speech. Mao had tried, by coercion, to create an equal society. He had driven the intellectuals out to farms. He had caused chaos late in his career. And Deng Xiaoping, at great cost to himself — he was imprisoned three times by the state — was arguing that what they were doing was against the way people function. In his most famous speech he said, "Look, I don't care if it's a black cat or a white cat; I care that it catches mice." And what he was saying was revolutionary. He was saying to the Communist Party of China, "Don't come in here and lecture me about ideology. Capitalism works and if we don't give the people of China jobs, if we don't give the people of China hope, they are going to throw us out and there will be a bloody revolution."

He spent twenty years getting the message across — he risked his life. And while I have many, many problems with the Chinese dictatorship, there are few achievements since World War II that have helped more human beings than the implementation of capitalism and the opening of markets in China. And I'd rather see those 600 million Chinese rise in a society with inequality than see them smothered in a society of absolute equality.

RUDYARD GRIFFITHS: Paul Krugman, you get the final word.

PAUL KRUGMAN: At the moment I am feeling that there have been so many straw men thrown out here tonight that we have created a fire hazard in this auditorium.

No one is advocating a society of complete equality — no one in this group, at any rate. It's nothing like that. And since I do spend a lot of time on the eurozone crisis, I want to say a word on that issue. If you think that excessive government is the problem in Europe, then how does Ireland prove your point? Ireland has famously low tax rates, especially for corporations across Europe — a zero percent tax rate in the case of Apple. Conservatives all around hailed Ireland as a role model — "a shining model," said George Osborne before he became chancellor of the exchequer in the United Kingdom. And Ireland is rather a mess now also, you know. They're not quite as bad as Greece, but that's not a slogan you want to run on — "Not quite as bad as Greece."

But that's not what this is about. With a former

Speaker of the House here, I, of all people, shouldn't have to be the one saying "Politics is the art of the possible." Policy is the art of the possible. We're not going to turn the United States into Cuba. What we might do — hopefully — is something like what President Obama has suggested in his last several budgets, which is closing more loopholes that the rich take advantage of, raising more revenue, possibly pushing top marginal rates higher. That's what I'd like to do.

What I take from Art Laffer is that the two great sins of recent history are: (1) the 2003 Bush tax cuts, which gave special treatment to dividend income and (2) the cut in the capital gains tax rate in the '90s that was under somebody's leadership in the House — I can't quite remember who *(he turns teasingly to Gingrich)*. I'd certainly like to abolish those cuts. I want to raise a few extra points of income from the top one percent and use that money for important things. I don't think that is going to solve all of our problems. I think it's a start toward reducing the excessive power of the elite. The fact of the matter is that in the past when we had more progressive taxation — when we came out of the 1930s with a much more progressive tax system than we had before — we also came out with a society that wasn't quite as plutocratic as it had been before. And that I'd like to do.

I will say one thing. I am not worried about us sliding back into the Gilded Age. We have slid back already. It has already happened. What we want to do now is claw our way back toward the kind of middle-class society we used to be.

RUDYARD GRIFFITHS: Well, gentlemen, a superb and hard-fought debate that has given us a lot to think about and to reflect on. Let's face it, the last few weeks here in the city of Toronto have not been great ones for the quality of public debate or, frankly, the quality of executive leadership. So you've given us a nice respite from that. And look, in all seriousness, I think events like this, and countless others in the city, remind us that — despite what happens in City Hall, despite an international reputation that we may have to start to unwind — we are a city of sophistication, we are a city of substance, we are a city of civility. We thank Peter and Melanie Munk for reminding us. Thank you.

Now for a crucial part of tonight's program: we are going to quickly review the audience vote at the start of the evening. We began tonight with strong support for the motion. Let's get those numbers up. Be it resolved: tax the rich more: 58 percent were in favour, 28 percent opposed, 14 percent undecided. As for the number of you that would change your mind over the course of the evening — I like Newt Gingrich's remark that 21 percent of you were absolutely adamant, you weren't budging — let's see whether you have budged or not. Each one of you has a second ballot in your program. Vote once and please use that vote wisely. And for those of you watching online, the show continues; it's not over. Our webcam town hall starts now on Spreecast, so share your analysis of the debate with fellow experts and with one another. Ladies and gentlemen, thanks for another great Munk Debate. Let's vote!

Summary: The pre-debate vote was 58 percent in favour of the resolution; 28 percent against; and 14 percent of voters were undecided. The final vote showed a disappearance of the undecided voters, with 70 percent in favour of the motion and 30 percent against it. Given the shift in votes, the victory goes to the team arguing for the resolution, Paul Krugman and George Papandreou.

NEWT GINGRICH IN CONVERSATION
WITH HOWARD GREEN

HOWARD GREEN: "Tax the rich" is the popular rallying cry of many among the middle class while the one percenters continue to race ahead. But hold on. Could making the rich pay more in taxes actually leave the economy and government coffers worse off as the wealthy look for new and clever ways to avoid taxes rather than growing their businesses? These two views took centre stage at this year's spring Munk Debate, an event that brings in top economic thinkers, orators, and intellectual curmudgeons from around the world. At this debate, Paul Krugman, Nobel Prize–winning economist and *New York Times* columnist, and former Greek prime minister George Papandreou argued for the affirmative, that the rich should be taxed more. Arguing for the other side, who said "hands off," were Newt Gingrich, former Speaker of the U.S. House of Representatives who unsuccessfully ran as the Republican nominee for president, and Arthur Laffer, the so-called "father" of supply-side economics and key economic adviser to President Ronald Reagan in the 1980s. I spoke with three of these economic heavy hitters: Krugman, Laffer, and, my first guest, Newt Gingrich.

Mr. Speaker, thank you for joining us. So, the resolution, "Be it resolved: tax the rich more." Why not?

NEWT GINGRICH: Good to be here.

I would respond with a question: Why? I mean, I understand everybody likes theft, and everybody likes the idea of getting somebody else's, but I think about it like this: Let's say you live in a neighbourhood, and you drive a mid-size car, which is okay. But your next-door neighbour has a really cool car. So, should you be able to take it? Well, why not? You want it; you've always wanted it.

HOWARD GREEN: Is it that simple?

NEWT GINGRICH: Well, just look at the wording of the resolution. It doesn't say "in a national emergency, when we're desperate for resources;" it doesn't say "at a time when we have some reason to do it." It's an objective. How much more? Should we confiscate Bill Gates's wealth? After all, why does he need all those billions?

HOWARD GREEN: Confiscate is a strong word.

NEWT GINGRICH: Isn't that what government does? It takes. Government is force. Government isn't charity;

government isn't "Gee, it would be nice if you wanted to help us." The two wealthiest Americans are worth something in the order of $90 billion between them. So, should we take from them? Leave them each a billion. After all, if they have a billion, they can't complain. It's still an awful lot of money — probably too much money, say our socialist friends. But do you think that we'd have as many people trying to become successful?

HOWARD GREEN: Warren Buffett — I'm sure you're referring to him as one of the two — he wants to be taxed more, at least he says so.

NEWT GINGRICH: Yes, I'm talking about Gates and Buffett. Buffett says he wants to be taxed more, and then he puts $30 billion into a tax-free foundation. Buffett's a very clever man.

I'm just saying that if you walked in this morning and said, "We've decided that a billion dollars is the most anyone should have, what rational reason is there to have more than a billion dollars?" Do you think that would increase the economic growth of the world, or decrease it? And we have a test case — China. The Chinese said, "We're going to go out, and we're going to create dramatic opportunities for people to become very, very, very wealthy." And in the process they've taken 600 million people into the middle class — the largest increase of the middle class in history. Now, are you willing to have a few billionaires if you're going to move 600 million people into the middle class?

HOWARD GREEN: But what about the reverse of that, say the middle class of the United States? A lot of people argue that the middle class in the United States — and here, for that matter — is under great pressure. Their economic well-being is eroding and economic inequality is widening between the middle class and the one percent. How do you address that?

NEWT GINGRICH: The greatest pressure on the middle class is a bad economy. When you have dramatic economic growth, when incomes are going up, when you need workers, people get better deals — not to mention it's easier to start a new business and be an entrepreneur. Remember, in most generations much of the new wealth is from the very first generation — people who created something brand new, who went out and did something different. Again, Bill Gates would be a perfect example. He wasn't born rich. I think when you have a rising economy, the middle class and the poor both do better. I mean, it's the momentum of the economy. As John F. Kennedy said, "The rising tide lifts all boats." John F. Kennedy was someone who was a very early supply-side advocate, which says something about the Democratic Party today; that JFK would be in a lot of trouble if he were serving in the current administration.

HOWARD GREEN: What about the marginal tax rates that the United States had in the Eisenhower days or the Kennedy days, which were at 90 percent and 70 percent, respectively. The United States was a very prosperous economy at the time with those high rates. Why wouldn't it be now?

NEWT GINGRICH: The hidden fact is if your income is premised only on capital gains, you pay half the marginal rate, which is true even in Canada. So if you're really wealthy, you put all of your income into capital gains. This is what happened with Mitt Romney. You end up with a dramatically lower marginal tax rate legally — no cheating — because you're clever. Well, guess what? Really wealthy people can hire really smart accountants and really smart tax lawyers. So, when you have a 70 percent marginal rate, people are looking for ways to conceal their money.

HOWARD GREEN: But does everyone work just for the money? I want to get to the incentive part of all of this because people who are extraordinarily rich are often extremely driven people; they want to prove something, they're working for more than just money.

NEWT GINGRICH: They're often extremely generous. Look at the size of the Gates Foundation; look at Andrew Carnegie, who built 2,200 libraries around the world. Carnegie is the largest single developer of libraries in history. Even look at philanthropists who give millions and millions of dollars to museums or to symphony orchestras or to universities.

HOWARD GREEN: There are a lot who don't, though, too.

NEWT GINGRICH: Right, but the question is do you want to live in a free society, where you encourage people to be generous, or do you want to live in a society where you take it away from them and eliminate the right to choose?

HOWARD GREEN: I'm sure you're even more familiar with this quote than I am, given that you're American and I'm Canadian, but can you comment on Oliver Wendell Holmes's famous quote: "Taxes are what we pay for civilized society?"

NEWT GINGRICH: Sure. I believe in taxes, but the question becomes how big does government need to be? How good is your government? One of the quotes I saw recently stated that the difference in the cost of a television set and health care has shifted by a factor of one hundred, meaning that televisions have become dramatically cheaper and health care has become dramatically more expensive. Guess which one is defined by government? Higher education suffers from the same problem. The more government interferes with our education, the more loans students accumulate, the more grants we amass, the more expensive higher education has become. At times, higher education has actually risen in cost faster than health care.

HOWARD GREEN: How do you explain the fact that the marginal tax rate has dropped significantly from that era, the 1950s and 1960s, to what it is now, yet the public debt is so much higher?

NEWT GINGRICH: We spend more than we take in. I mean, it's not complicated. I helped lead the effort with President Clinton to get the only four consecutively balanced budgets in modern American history, and we did it by controlling spending. We actually cut taxes to accelerate economic growth, and for four straight years we had a balanced budget. So, the way you get to a balanced budget is in part — and every family knows this — by controlling your spending. Countries are like giant families.

HOWARD GREEN: So, what's the answer? What's the right rate of taxation?

NEWT GINGRICH: I think the right answer is a flat tax that's very clean, very simple, and easy to administer. I also want it to be fair in the sense that if you're a millionaire, you'd pay dramatically more than if you were someone who earned a very small income. If you earned $20,000 — then let's say it's a 10 percent flat tax. And you'd probably have an exemption per person, so you wouldn't take anything before you're at $40,000 or $50,000 of income to allow people to exempt the first layer of their revenue. So, if you're making $50,000 and you're taxed a 10 percent flat rate, you would pay $5,000. If you're a millionaire, you'd be paying $990,000. Under a flat-tax system, the person making more money is paying exactly the same percentage as the person making less, but contributing dramatically more cash. I think in that sense you're getting a lot more money out of them.

HOWARD GREEN: You've put this idea forward and so have Arthur Laffer and Steve Forbes — a lot of people have proposed it. But if it's so logical, why doesn't it gain any traction?

NEWT GINGRICH: I think there are a lot of people who'd like to see it passed. I think that there are a lot of technical reasons that make it hard in the United States. But there are countries that have adopted it, where it has worked very well; Russia and Estonia have both adopted it.

HOWARD GREEN: Is Russia a good example, though? With a flat tax, they still stuff their money in banks in Cyprus!

NEWT GINGRICH: But the Russians, in fact, had a dramatic increase in economic growth when they went to a flat tax.

HOWARD GREEN: So, failing that happening, it seems like it's very difficult to make any changes at the present time in Washington — I don't have to tell you that. What do you do about the lack of infrastructure in the United States and Canada? Both countries need to make massive improvements to their infrastructure to repair the country; both have an aging demographic that is going to need more health care — we're all going to need more succour in our old age. How do you pay for all of that if you can't reform the tax system?

NEWT GINGRICH: First of all, I would argue that it's amazing how little time is spent trying to figure out how to make government less expensive. It's very easy to walk around and say, "Gee, this is all so expensive, let's take somebody else's taxes." But in reality, how are we going to pay for the examples you just used? I think if we open up federal land for development of oil and gas in the United States, the royalties that would come into the federal government could fund infrastructure development with no tax increase.

HOWARD GREEN: Even with all of the pushback about things like Keystone XL, which we're trying to get approval for in the United States?

NEWT GINGRICH: That's a political fight, not an infrastructure fight. And one of the reasons it hasn't been approved is because the Sierra Club is opposed to Canadian oil. I hope the president's going to approve it; I've advocated approving the pipeline. If you look at all of America's oil and gas potential, a great deal of which is on federal land, some of which is offshore, we're in a position where it could produce something like $50 billion a year in additional royalties for the federal government with no tax increase. Now, if you allocated half of that to deficit reduction and half of that to infrastructure, you'd have an enormous infrastructure program.

HOWARD GREEN: Just bringing it back to the resolution, and an offshoot of it, are you concerned with what appears to be growing inequality and a widening of incomes among people?

NEWT GINGRICH: I think there's an interesting question because when you measure individuals, you don't see any great increase in inequality. What's happening is —

HOWARD GREEN: Sorry, can you explain that?

NEWT GINGRICH: Economists always look at families, but families have changed very dramatically. So, they used to measure a certain kind of family structure. Now you're measuring people who may be single as opposed to people who may have two working members of the household. All of those are listed as families. Family structure in both Canada and the United States has changed very dramatically.

HOWARD GREEN: But real wages have not really gone up for thirty years in either country.

NEWT GINGRICH: But that's a factor of competition, frankly, particularly in relation to China. And I think you're going to see wages go up. If you look at North Dakota today, for example, wages have skyrocketed. They actually have a negative unemployment rate; that is, they have 2.3 percent more jobs than they have people filling them. Look at parts of western

Canada — you have the same thing going on. If we had a government in the United States that favoured economic development and that didn't have a constant regulatory and litigation fight against economic development, you'd see wages going up, you'd see jobs created, and you'd see a country that has a lot more revenue with no tax increase.

HOWARD GREEN: So, I'm assuming you would not like to see a carbon tax, then.

NEWT GINGRICH: No. I think a carbon tax is very anti-poor and very anti-development. And I think that's a very negative approach to get to a better future.

HOWARD GREEN: What about a national consumption tax? That's a flat tax, which we have here in Canada.

NEWT GINGRICH: In the United States we have consumption taxes in most states — they're called sales taxes — and they're collected at the state and local level. And there's been deep opposition to the federal government pre-empting what's been a major source of income at the state and local level.

HOWARD GREEN: But what about a national tax to deal with your deficit and debt problems?

NEWT GINGRICH: I think you deal with the deficit and debt by cutting spending. I don't think America is a country that's under-taxed; I think America is a country that's over-governed.

HOWARD GREEN: Would you still like to be president of the United States?

NEWT GINGRICH: Sure. It'd be an extraordinary challenge. I think we're entering a period where we're going to break out in technology and break out in science, and I believe the next twenty years could be among the most exciting in human history, so it'd be great to be part of that process.

HOWARD GREEN: Are you going to run again in 2016?

NEWT GINGRICH: I don't know yet, but we're certainly looking at it.

HOWARD GREEN: If you run and win, will you do an interview with me after?

NEWT GINGRICH: *(Laughing)* We'll try to work you in; we could do it at the Keystone Pipeline, which will hopefully be completed by then.

HOWARD GREEN: *(Laughing)* Okay, great to have you with us. That was Newt Gingrich, the former Speaker of the U.S. House of Representatives.

PAUL KRUGMAN IN CONVERSATION
WITH HOWARD GREEN

HOWARD GREEN: We just heard from former U.S. House Speaker Newt Gingrich, who argued that taxing the rich more would leave the economy worse off, but Nobel Prize–winning economist and Princeton professor Paul Krugman disagrees. He says higher taxes on the rich are necessary. Great to have you back with us, Paul, many thanks.

PAUL KRUGMAN: Good to be here again.

HOWARD GREEN: So, the debate on whether to tax the rich more or not. Give us a précis of your argument. Why should the rich — the super rich — pay more taxes?

PAUL KRUGMAN: First of all, because we could use the money. You don't even have to get into a grand ideological debate or an argument about the effect of the greater concentration of wealth and income on our society, though I think those are important issues. The first thing to say right away is that we live in a time when we're worried about paying for essential government services and at the same time, we have tax rates on the wealthy — certainly in the United States and, to a large extent, in other advanced countries, including Canada — that are well below levels they've been at in the past. And evidence suggests that a significant amount of money can be raised by going partway back toward those old levels of taxes, with no adverse economic effects. I have nothing against rich people. I just think that we want more of their money so that we can pay for all of the things we need.

HOWARD GREEN: Is it the best way to raise the revenue that governments need?

PAUL KRUGMAN: It is a way to raise the revenue. Governments need to raise revenue in a variety of ways. I think the right way to think about this is what kinds of things are we doing in an attempt to save money, while raising some additional money by having somewhat higher taxes on the wealthy? And the numbers are actually quite stunning.

There is a debate that we're having right now in the U.S. legislature involving food stamps. A number of people in Congress are saying that we have to cut the food stamp program because it's too much money — they want to cut $20 billion in the next ten years. Meanwhile, the top one percent of income earners in the United States have a combined income of something like $1 trillion a year.

HOWARD GREEN: Income, not assets?

PAUL KRUGMAN: Income — $1 trillion of income per year, which is $10 trillion over the next ten years. So, we are really saying that we cannot afford $20 billion in nutritional aid to desperately poor families because we dare not raise the tax rate by that fraction of a percent on that one percent that would allow us to pay for this.

HOWARD GREEN: What about the argument that people on the other side make — if I can put it that way — that the more you raise the marginal rate, the more incentive there is for rich people to hire more tax accountants and lawyers to find ways to avoid paying those taxes?

PAUL KRUGMAN: We've done a lot of study on that. This is not a subject for idle speculation. Economists have done very, very careful studies that have looked at what actually happens when top tax rates change.

HOWARD GREEN: But people on the other side of this argument have done studies, too.

PAUL KRUGMAN: As a matter of fact they haven't. If you look at the people who've actually done the work, who have looked at the data to see what they tell us, the studies have been quite uniform. Yes, there is some effect on behaviour of the one percent; there is some actual tax avoidance. The reported income of the wealthy does fall somewhat when top tax rates go up, but it doesn't fall by very much. And if we're asking what the tax rate is that would maximize revenue, at what point does raising taxes actually become counterproductive in terms of revenue? It's at a number that is at least 70 percent, probably 80 percent.

HOWARD GREEN: Marginal tax rate?

PAUL KRUGMAN: Marginal tax rate.

HOWARD GREEN: So, back to the rates of the 1950s and 1960s.

PAUL KRUGMAN: That's right. I mean this is not going to actually happen, right? But ideally moving in that direction — certainly not where tax levels are right now.

HOWARD GREEN: I believe it would astound a lot of people that you are arguing we could implement a marginal tax rate of 70 to 80 percent for high-income earners and have no sort of erosion in revenues and no increase in tax avoidance.

PAUL KRUGMAN: No, you would have an increase in avoidance, but the question is how much? And remember that you're raising tax rates on people; they will have to achieve a lot of avoidance for that avoidance to offset the fact that you are collecting money on the stuff that you can catch.

HOWARD GREEN: Like Gérard Depardieu in France, for instance? Seventy-five percent tax rate raise and he's off to Russia.

PAUL KRUGMAN: Has he actually moved yet, though? My understanding is that there's a lot more talk about moving to other places than there is actual movement. We have a lot of experience; over the years in the United States, we've had tax rates on the rich that have varied a lot over time. And so we're not flying blind here. We've got a lot of evidence on what actually happens when you implement a higher tax rate, and those studies don't find the kind of massive evasion that people claim we need to be worried about.

HOWARD GREEN: Let me ask you about something your opposition says. They argue that you remove incentives when you take away financial reward. You erode the value of work.

PAUL KRUGMAN: I'm a card-carrying economist, so I have to believe that incentives matter. And they do matter, but the question is how much do they matter in this range? Look, in the United States we went through a long period, a quarter century after World War II, with top tax rates that were way higher than they are now. In fact, way higher than anybody would consider proposing right now. And yet that was also the most successful generation of economic growth in our country's history.

HOWARD GREEN: Were there other factors at play?

PAUL KRUGMAN: Most of the explanations people try to use don't make sense. The fact of the matter is, at that time we had a vigorous growing economy with tax rates that, according to modern ideological prejudices, should have totally killed incentives. It's also important to mention that if we look at our economy right now, the highest actual marginal tax rates — the de facto marginal tax rates — are not on the wealthy. They are actually on lower-income working people who see means-tested benefits go away as their income goes up. So, if you're really worried about incentives, that's where you should focus. And the fact of the matter is, even with higher tax rates there, we're a pretty hard-working people. So I think the point is not that incentives don't matter. However, I find it interesting and ultimately self-serving that people suggest that somehow the rich will be uniquely discouraged from doing great things for the rest of us if we raise the income tax rate.

HOWARD GREEN: Let's talk about the concept of redistribution. I guess some people would ask why should those who earn a lot redistribute to others who may not work as hard, may not have studied as hard, invented things, and what not?

PAUL KRUGMAN: The short answer is — and I believe Louis Brandeis said it — taxes are the price of civilization.

HOWARD GREEN: Oliver Wendell Holmes said it, I think.

PAUL KRUGMAN: Okay, Oliver Wendell Holmes. Anyway, taxes are the price of civilization. We live in a society; none of us is an island. All of us need to preserve the basics of civilization. All of us, really, should feel an obligation to contribute what is necessary. To think, "This is mine, I alone am entitled to it" is wrong. Of course we want hard work rewarded, we want innovation rewarded, and our society provides lots of rewards for all of that. But we should also say, be grateful that we live in an advanced country, with advanced infrastructure, with a social safety net that helps keep us a decent society, which we all want to live in. And, because the rich are more able to pay to provide those things, they should pay a somewhat higher share of their income in taxes than those who are less well off. To make this a huge moral issue is, I think, to just imagine that you live in a kind of society that has never existed.

HOWARD GREEN: So, what about the notion of a flat tax, which your opponents in the debate will no doubt bring up. Arthur Laffer believes it should be 6.5 percent, Newt Gingrich says 10 percent. What do you think of the concept?

PAUL KRUGMAN: The math never works. Any flat tax that

provides the services that the public, in fact, demands is going to be a much higher tax rate than flat-tax advocates are ever willing to admit. They always want to make it seem as if ordinary middle-class families will be paying no more than they are now; that it's all going to be great; that they're going to be able to keep their retirement programs, and their health care programs, and you know, their other government services. And the truth is you can't raise enough money for those things without either having the middle class pay a substantially higher tax than it now does, or having a progressive tax system that levies substantially higher rates on the truly wealthy.

HOWARD GREEN: So, then, back to an appropriate marginal rate. Would you be an advocate of going as high as 70 or 80 percent?

PAUL KRUGMAN: At the very highest levels, yes. It's pretty straightforward.

HOWARD GREEN: What would the highest levels be? Where would you set the income bar for the highest level of taxation?

PAUL KRUGMAN: It's probably in the million-plus income range — maybe even higher than that. It would take some figuring out to get there. But look, in a way it's idle speculation because we know politically, we ain't going there, right? The only real question now is whether we're going to move some distance in that direction. The math really pushes you toward saying that for very high incomes, multi-million-dollar incomes, the marginal rate — not the average, but the marginal tax rate — should be in the vicinity of 70 percent.

HOWARD GREEN: What about other forms of taxation? What about a carbon tax?

PAUL KRUGMAN: I'm for that, too. And to the extent that it can yield us a significant amount of revenue, which is a good thing, although that's not the main reason to do it.

HOWARD GREEN: What do you think the likelihood is that a carbon tax will actually happen, given that President Obama highlighted climate change as one of his priorities in his State of the Union address?

PAUL KRUGMAN: We're going to need a couple of wave elections before anything like that happens. At the moment it's just inconceivable, so you have to either have a complete turnover of control in the House of Representatives, or a conversion experience on the part of the Republican Party before we get to that point.

HOWARD GREEN: Associated with a catastrophic environmental effect?

PAUL KRUGMAN: Hopefully not. I certainly would like to imagine that as a species we have enough wisdom to act before that happens. But yes, I mean, in the end it's likely that we will have carbon taxes. In the end we're going to have to control carbon, and might as well raise revenue in the process. It's very likely that the United States will also eventually have some sort of a value-added tax as well. Running a modern state is expensive, and we're simply going to need more revenue. It can't all come from the wealthy, but some of it should come from the wealthy.

HOWARD GREEN: What is the political likelihood, in the next couple of election cycles, that you would have a value-added tax, a consumption tax like we have here?

PAUL KRUGMAN: That might be closer than you might think. I guess we have to ask ourselves how many Democrats does Hillary Clinton pull in in her big 2016 victory, and then we'll talk.

HOWARD GREEN: You think she's going to run and you think she could win?

PAUL KRUGMAN: I don't know. I have no insider information whatsoever on whether she's going to run. I think if she does run, she's going to win.

HOWARD GREEN: What about you? No doubt you have a reasonably high income yourself — a Nobel Prize winner, among other achievements. Do you like paying more taxes?

PAUL KRUGMAN: I don't like paying more taxes. Basically everything I advocate is to my personal financial disadvantage. I'm very much in the range where the kinds of things we're talking about would hurt me and would reduce my income, but it comes back to what I was saying earlier — we live in a society. I want to live in a society that I consider a decent society, and I am willing to pay higher taxes as the price of that society.

HOWARD GREEN: Great to have you back with us.

PAUL KRUGMAN: Thank you.

ARTHUR LAFFER IN CONVERSATION
WITH HOWARD GREEN

HOWARD GREEN: So, you just heard Paul Krugman explain why higher taxes on the rich are necessary. Now, my interview with Arthur Laffer, the "father" of supply-side economics and economic adviser to former U.S. president Ronald Reagan. Arthur, good to have you back with us.

ARTHUR LAFFER: Thank you, it's a pleasure.

HOWARD GREEN: So, "Be it resolved: tax the rich more." Why not?

ARTHUR LAFFER: Well, number one, they won't pay it. I mean, you'll lose money if you try. These guys have all sorts of ways of avoiding taxes. They can change the volume of their income, they can change the location of their income, they can change the composition of their income, and they can change the timing of it. And they can hire all the lawyers and accountants and different income specialists and lobbyists around the world, so if higher tax advocates think they're going to get their money, I don't think they're right. And every time we've raised tax rates on the rich in the United States over a period of time, we've lost their money.

HOWARD GREEN: Can you change the rules, though, to capture the avoidance?

ARTHUR LAFFER: That's what I'd like to do. I'd like to change the rules totally. I'm all for taxing the rich more, but not with higher tax rates. I think we should get rid of the deductions, exemptions, exclusions, and make it so that all income is taxed at one flat rate, and then these guys will pay their fair share.

HOWARD GREEN: And that flat rate would be?

ARTHUR LAFFER: I did it for Jerry Brown when he ran for president. We had it at a little less than 12 percent, assuming we did a value-added tax and a personal unadjusted income tax and got rid of all federal taxes in the United States — all of them. I want to get rid of income tax, corporate tax, all payroll taxes, Medicare, Medicaid taxes, capital gains and estate taxes, tariffs, all of it. You get rid of all of that and you tax value-added once at 12 percent and personal unadjusted gross income at 12 percent and that comes out to about 24 percent of GDP. There are some items you can't tax like the imputed profits of government corporations and stuff, but can you imagine? You wouldn't even have to file a tax return! You wouldn't have to worry about the IRS —

HOWARD GREEN: Is life that simple, though?

ARTHUR LAFFER: No, but economics is.

HOWARD GREEN: It is?

ARTHUR LAFFER: Sure, of course it is. Look at what we did in 1986. We dropped the highest rate from 50 percent to 28 percent. And we raised the lowest rate. We went from fourteen tax brackets to four brackets. That wasn't exactly what I'm talking about now, but we dropped the corporate rate from 46 percent to 34 percent, and we got it passed in the Senate with ninety-seven out of one hundred votes.

HOWARD GREEN: But look at how much debt the United States is carrying now.

ARTHUR LAFFER: Well, that wasn't because of the tax of '86, come on. It's because of all the screw-ups since then. And it's because of the wars, and it's because of bad tax systems, it's because of poverty. The stimulus spending has resulted in heavy taxes. And everyone believes these taxes stimulate the economy, but I believe this government spending is taxation.

HOWARD GREEN: But what would you have done after the financial crisis?

ARTHUR LAFFER: Let it go.

HOWARD GREEN: Let it go?

ARTHUR LAFFER: Yes. It didn't destroy one car. It wouldn't destroy one building or one human.

HOWARD GREEN: You think the auto industry would've survived without the stimulus spending? They were bankrupt.

ARTHUR LAFFER: Well, I don't know whether the auto industry would have survived, but the question is should the auto industry survive as it is now?

HOWARD GREEN: They're making a profit again.

ARTHUR LAFFER: (Scoffs and laughs)

HOWARD GREEN: No?

ARTHUR LAFFER: Yes, after subsidies, but Solyndra probably would have someday, too.

HOWARD GREEN: *(Laughs)*

ARTHUR LAFFER: There you go! Go for it, Bureau of Motor Vehicles!

HOWARD GREEN: I'm getting myself into trouble here. Back to taxes. Paul Krugman says a flat tax — the math — just doesn't work.

ARTHUR LAFFER: I just told you the math does work. Who are you going to believe? Him or me? I just told you the exact numbers. I mean, these are calculated. Jerry Brown ran on this system as a Democrat in '92 and almost beat Bill Clinton in the primary. I did all of his flat-tax numbers. It's not just a Republican thing.

HOWARD GREEN: It didn't work for Steve Forbes, though.

ARTHUR LAFFER: Steve Forbes didn't propose a complete flat-tax system; he just proposed a flat income tax. You know, you can't cure part of the tax system and let the rest go. You've got to cure the whole system. One of the big problems is this bits-and-pieces stuff. That's why when you raise rates, you're diddling with the tax codes. You really just want to do a complete overhaul. All the problems with this complicated tax code are obvious. I'm sure if the IRS came after anyone in the United States, they could find something wrong with how they've calculated their taxes. That's not the way it should be. It should be that everyone could do his or her own tax returns. And that the companies you work for collect your taxes. If your employer owes you a hundred bucks, they would give you eighty-eight bucks, and send twelve to the government. The same would be true if you mowed someone's lawn for ten bucks — you would send in $1.20. The bulk of all this stuff is just income taxes and it shouldn't be differentiated by the amount of money you make.

HOWARD GREEN: Back to the whole question of income inequality and whether the rich should be taxed more or not . . .

ARTHUR LAFFER: But they should be taxed more.

HOWARD GREEN: They should be taxed more?

ARTHUR LAFFER: Not higher rates!

HOWARD GREEN: But in absolute terms?

ARTHUR LAFFER: Let me give you an example. In his *New York Times* letter, Warren Buffett said that he paid a little less than $7 million in taxes. His tax rate was 17.4 percent, which put his taxable income at roughly a little under $40 million. That's a lot of money. But in that same year, his wealth increased by $10 billion in unrealized capital gains, which are not taxed. He gave $1.6 billion to the Bill and Melinda Gates Foundation in that year. But his total income was over $12 billion.

HOWARD GREEN: You're talking about calculating income differently?

ARTHUR LAFFER: Yes! You tax all forms of income at a low rate — a flat tax. You also tax gifts and get rid of 501(c)(3)s.

HOWARD GREEN: What's a 501(c)(3)?

ARTHUR LAFFER: Tax-exempt organizations like universities, health clinics, all of these political operations.

HOWARD GREEN: Universities are political operations?

ARTHUR LAFFER: No. I said also including political operations. Of course you should tax universities. Why should their gifts be tax-exempt?

HOWARD GREEN: What about the marginal tax rates that existed in the United States in the 1950s and 1960s? Those rates were around 90 percent, then they went down to 70 percent, but they were still very high. It was also at a time when the United States was perhaps at its strongest, economically.

ARTHUR LAFFER: There are three things that matter about that issue. One is how much you spend in tax. And back in those days, we spent much less than we do now. Two is how you collect your taxes — they did have much higher rates then. And my third point is how you spend your money because that also matters. In very simple terms, if you tax people who work and you pay people who don't work, don't be surprised if you find a lot of people not working. These are three things we need to ask ourselves today. When John F. Kennedy became president, he cut the highest rate from 91 percent to 70 percent. He said, quite correctly, that it was the tax rates that were holding America back, and then we had the go-go '60s.

HOWARD GREEN: At 70 percent.

ARTHUR LAFFER: But down from 91. Yes, it would have been great to get it down to 12 percent back then, but he didn't. Kennedy did drop it down from 91 percent, which was hurting the country, to 70 percent, which was hurting it a lot less. And you got this economic boom. And then you got the Four Stooges — Johnson, Nixon, Ford, and Carter. They raised taxes, and revenues from the rich went down. Revenues from the rich under Kennedy went way up as a share of GDP. You know, if you want to collect money from people, make sure they pay the taxes instead of finding loopholes.

HOWARD GREEN: A lot of people talk about the incentives side of it. Tax people more and they will lose the incentive to work. But, correct me if I'm wrong, a lot of people who are rich or who run companies are the most incentivized people on earth because it comes from something internal within them. They're driven. They want to prove something.

ARTHUR LAFFER: They're competitive, how about that?

HOWARD GREEN: You could probably pay them a lot less.

ARTHUR LAFFER: Yes, I'm sure you could pay a lot of them less. But I'll tell you, if they could figure out a way to make more, they'd do it. And that's the problem — they're smart and they can also hire lawyers.

HOWARD GREEN: But would they work less if you taxed them more?

ARTHUR LAFFER: I'm not saying they would work less. It's not a matter of whether they work more or less. If you tax job creators at higher rates, do you think they're going to create more jobs? No!

HOWARD GREEN: But they have something to prove; they have a desire to achieve that comes from within; they are driven —

ARTHUR LAFFER: People will do all sorts of things. But I'll tell you, all of them — every single one — will try to get around the taxes. And they will go to great lengths to do it. Now maybe you consider trying to become a tax dodger work, but I don't. I'd rather have the rich focusing on their businesses than focusing on their taxes. That's why I like a low-rate flat tax: let them get to work and make great products for us to consume cheaply.

HOWARD GREEN: So, let me turn the corner a bit. You know, flat-tax proposals have been around for a while, and they have not been adopted.

ARTHUR LAFFER: What do you mean by that? They've been adopted everywhere.

HOWARD GREEN: Well, no, not income tax in the United States.

ARTHUR LAFFER: Well, Massachusetts has a flat tax, Russia, Hong Kong —

HOWARD GREEN: We don't have it here and we don't have it in the United States federally, right?

ARTHUR LAFFER: No we don't, but we're moving closer to it —

HOWARD GREEN: Let me interject. If you want to have that kind of proposal that you are advocating, how do you reduce income inequality?

ARTHUR LAFFER: By creating jobs. I'll just quote Kennedy on this: "The best form of welfare is still a good high-paying job." And, you know, what Benjamin Hook said, which I loved — blacks are hired last and fired first. The only way they're ever going to get jobs and keep them is if there are so many damn jobs around, they have to be hired. There's no alternative to economic growth or prosperity. You want income equality at zero, but I don't. I would much rather have everyone richer, even if some are a little bit richer than others. I like to create jobs and reduce poverty — that's my dream. But I have no problem with rich people. I have a problem with poverty. I want to see poor people become rich.

HOWARD GREEN: But Reaganomics was known as trickle-down economics, and the criticism is that very little trickled down.

ARTHUR LAFFER: That's just plain not true. Every income category in the quintile went up in income. Yes, some went up higher. But the real change in the distribution of income — of all your Gini coefficients — occurred in the late '80s, not at the beginning of the growth period. Between 1982 and 1985, the United States had massive growth. Income distributions didn't get out of line until much later — under Clinton, I might add. I voted for Clinton twice, just so you know.

HOWARD GREEN: I read that. But if the tax code does not change, if there's stasis in the United States and you continue to carry these high deficits, debts, and so forth, how do you pay for necessary infrastructure changes? How do you pay for an aging demographic or health care for citizens?

ARTHUR LAFFER: It's really tough. How do you pay for something you can't afford? You know, that's the problem.

What I'd like to see us do is increase our income so that we can afford these things. But what you're telling me is, if you can't change the income, how can you afford these things? You can't!

HOWARD GREEN: I'm asking you, I'm not telling you.

ARTHUR LAFFER: No, I understand what you're asking, and the question is, we need economic growth to be able to afford any of these things you are talking about. How can a poor country afford good health care? How can it afford infrastructure spending? It can't. What you need to do is create prosperity. The most immoral act the government can perpetrate on its citizenry is to enact policies that have the effect of destroying the production base.

HOWARD GREEN: Are you worried about the potential for social unrest?

ARTHUR LAFFER: We already have it.

HOWARD GREEN: But more social unrest because of income inequality.

ARTHUR LAFFER: No, economic growth reduces social unrest. I mean, how many riots were there in America under Reagan? Major riots? Zero. In the preceding four presidencies? Lots. When people have good jobs, they can't afford to sit around and riot.

HOWARD GREEN: There were riots in Britain under Thatcher.

ARTHUR LAFFER: That's true. There is always the exception to the truth.

HOWARD GREEN: *(Laughs)*

ARTHUR LAFFER: I'm just teasing you. Yes, you are correct. But let's take Cameron. I love to use Britain as an example of this idea. Cameron comes in, raises the highest tax rate in the United Kingdom from 40 percent to 50 percent and what happened? A double-dip recession, and they didn't get more money. That's exactly what happens in these cases. You think Hollande is going to get a great result in France? I don't think so. I'm willing to bet against it. I think they're all doomed. They're all trying to be do-gooders, but they're really doing a lot of harm.

HOWARD GREEN: What about the quote by Oliver Wendell Holmes, your famous Supreme Court justice: "Taxes are what we pay for civilized society?"

ARTHUR LAFFER: He was a good man. I'm not against taxes. I'm just against high tax rates that people get around. To get a good tax system, you need to have very, very heavy voluntary compliance. And if people think your tax codes are unjust and unfair, they're going to try to get around them. No one minds paying taxes for a civilized society; they just don't want to be ripped off. And when you create tax codes the way governments are now, you are ripping people off, which is the problem. With a low flat-tax rate, everyone knows they have to contribute their fair share. And I don't mind taxing the rich a lot more. As I mentioned, if Warren Buffett paid a 12 percent flat tax, he'd have paid $1.4 billion in taxes instead of $6 million. His effective tax rate was six one-hundredths of one percent. That's not fair. But it's not because the rates weren't high enough, it's because the base wasn't broad enough, so let's develop the correct tax system that raises the requisite revenues to allow government to function properly, to create a civilized society. I'm very in favour of government projects and services as long as government is better at doing those things than the rest of the population. Government should implement a low flat-tax rate, spending restraints, sound money, free trade, minimal regulations; and if it can't do those things, then get out of the way and let the people solve their own problems.

HOWARD GREEN: Great to have you back.

ARTHUR LAFFER: Thank you. It was fun to be back.

HOWARD GREEN: Thanks a lot. Arthur Laffer, former economic adviser to U.S. President Ronald Reagan.

ACKNOWLEDGEMENTS

The Munk Debates are the product of the public-spiritedness of a remarkable group of civic-minded organizations and individuals. First and foremost, these debates would not be possible without the vision and leadership of the Aurea Foundation. Founded in 2006 by Peter and Melanie Munk, the Aurea Foundation supports Canadian individuals and institutions involved in the study and development of public policy. The debates are the foundation's signature initiative, a model for the kind of substantive public policy conversation Canadians can foster globally. Since their creation in 2008, the foundation has underwritten the entire cost of each semi-annual debate. The debates have also benefited from the input and advice of members of the board of the foundation, including Mark Cameron, Andrew Coyne, Devon Cross, Allan Gotlieb, George Jonas, Margaret MacMillan, Anthony Munk, and Janice Stein.

For her contribution to the preliminary edit of the book, the debate organizers would like to thank Jane McWhinney.

Since their inception the Munk Debates have sought to take the discussions that happen at each event to national and international audiences. Here the debates have benefited immeasurably from a partnership with Canada's national newspaper, the *Globe and Mail*, and the counsel of its editor-in-chief, John Stackhouse.

With the publication of this superb book, House of Anansi Press is helping the debates reach new audiences in Canada and internationally. The debates' organizers would like to thank Anansi chair, Scott Griffin, and president and publisher, Sarah MacLachlan, for their enthusiasm for this book project and insights into how to translate the spoken debate into a powerful written intellectual exchange.

ABOUT THE DEBATERS

PAUL KRUGMAN is an American economist and renowned columnist for the *New York Times*. He won the 2008 Nobel Prize in Economics for his groundbreaking work on international trade and economic geography. In addition to the Nobel Prize, Krugman's work in economics has earned him broad acclaim from the economic press and several prestigious awards, including the John Bates Clark Medal for his work on international trade and the 2011 Gerald Loeb Award for commentary. *Foreign Policy* magazine named Krugman one of its 2012 "Top 100 Global Thinkers." He has published over 200 scholarly articles and 20 books, including the most recent call to action, *End This Depression Now!* Professor Krugman also teaches economics and international affairs at Princeton, and is Centenary Professor at the London School of Economics.

GEORGE PAPANDREOU was the prime minister of Greece from 2009 to 2011. He is the current president of Socialist International. He was named one of *Foreign Policy* magazine's "Top 100 Global Thinkers" in 2010 for "making the best of Greece's worst year." Papandreou also held the portfolio of foreign minister from 1999 to 2004. He was a key player in the negotiations that led to Turkey's candidacy for membership in the European Union in 1999 and Cyprus's entry into the EU in 2004. He also held other government posts, including under-secretary for cultural affairs and minister for education. Following his grandfather Georgios Papandreou and his father, Andreas Papandreou, he was the third member of the Papandreou family to serve as the country's prime minister.

NEWT GINGRICH is a former Speaker of the U.S. House of Representatives, a *New York Times* bestselling author, and *Time* magazine's 1995 Man of the Year. Called "the indispensable leader" by the *Washington Times*, he was the architect of the Contract with America, which led the Republican Party to victory in 1994 by capturing the majority in the U.S. House of Representatives for the first time in forty years. Under his leadership, Congress passed welfare reform, the first balanced budget in a generation, and the first tax cut in sixteen years.

As an author, Gingrich has published twenty-four books, including fourteen fiction and non-fiction *New York Times* bestsellers. Non-fiction books include his latest, *A Nation Like No Other: Why American Exceptionalism*

Matters, as well as *To Save America: Stopping Obama's Secular-Socialist Machine.* Gingrich is also chair of the Gingrich Group, a communications and consulting firm that specializes in transformational change, with offices in Atlanta and Washington, D.C. In addition, he serves as a member of the Defense Policy Board and is on the Terrorism Task Force for the Council on Foreign Relations. He founded and chaired several policy think tanks, including American Solutions for Winning the Future and the Center for Health Transformation.

ARTHUR LAFFER is known as the "father" of supply-side economics. He was economic adviser to Ronald Reagan for both of his terms (1981–89), a member of the Reagan-Bush Finance Committee, and adviser to Margaret Thatcher on fiscal policy. One of his earliest successes in shaping public policy was his involvement in Proposition 13, the groundbreaking California initiative that drastically cut property taxes in the state in 1978.

A co-author of *The End of Prosperity: How Higher Taxes Will Doom the Economy — If We Let It Happen,* Dr. Laffer was listed by *Time* magazine as one of "The Century's Greatest Minds" for developing the Laffer Curve, a representation of the relationship between possible rates of taxation and the resulting levels of government revenue. The *Los Angeles Times* named him among "A Dozen Who Shaped the '80s," and he was featured in "A Gallery of the Greatest People Who Influenced Our Daily Business" in the *Wall Street Journal.*

He has also been a professor at Pepperdine University,

the University of Southern California, and the University of Chicago. He is the founder and chairman of Laffer Associates, an institutional economic research and consulting firm that focuses on the interconnecting macroeconomic, political, and demographic changes affecting global financial markets.

ABOUT THE EDITOR

RUDYARD GRIFFITHS is the organizer and moderator of the Munk Debates. In 2006 he was named one of Canada's "Top 40 under 40" by the *Globe and Mail*. He is the editor of thirteen books on history, politics, and international affairs, including *Who We Are: A Citizen's Manifesto*, which was a *Globe and Mail* Best Book of 2009 and a finalist for the Shaughnessy Cohen Prize for Political Writing. He lives in Toronto with his wife and two children.

ABOUT THE MUNK DEBATES

The Munk Debates are Canada's premier public policy event. Held semi-annually, the debates provide leading thinkers with a global forum to discuss the major public policy issues facing the world and Canada. Each event takes place in Toronto in front of a live audience, and the proceedings are covered by domestic and international media. Participants in recent Munk Debates include Robert Bell, Tony Blair, John Bolton, Ian Bremmer, Daniel Cohn-Bendit, Paul Collier, Howard Dean, Hernando de Soto, Gareth Evans, Mia Farrow, Niall Ferguson, William Frist, David Gratzer, Rick Hillier, Christopher Hitchens, Richard Holbrooke, Josef Joffe, Henry Kissinger, Charles Krauthammer, Paul Krugman, Lord Nigel Lawson, Stephen Lewis, David Li, Bjørn Lomborg, Lord Peter Mandelson, Elizabeth May, George Monbiot, Dambisa Moyo, Vali Nasr, Samantha Power, David Rosenberg, Lawrence Summers, Amos Yadlin, and Fareed Zakaria.

The Munk Debates are a project of the Aurea Foundation, a charitable organization established in 2006 by philanthropists Peter and Melanie Munk to promote public policy research and discussion. For more information, visit www.munkdebates.com.

ABOUT THE INTERVIEWS

Howard Green's interviews with Newt Gingrich, Paul Krugman, and Arthur Laffer were recorded on May 31, 2013, and aired on his show *Headline with Howard Green* on BNN. Zena Olijnyk produced the segments. BNN is gratefully acknowledged for permission to reprint excerpts from the following:

(p. 53) "Newt Gingrich in Conversation," by Howard Green. Copyright 2013 TBC. Transcribed by Maria Lioutaia.

(p. 65) "Paul Krugman in Conversation," by Howard Green. Copyright 2013 TBC. Transcribed by Maria Lioutaia.

(p. 77) "Arthur Laffer in Conversation," by Howard Green. Copyright 2013 TBC. Transcribed by Maria Lioutaia.

Can the World Tolerate an Iran with Nuclear Weapons?

Krauthammer and Yadlin vs. Zakaria and Nasr

Is the case for a pre-emptive strike on Iran ironclad? Or can a nuclear Iran be a stabilizing force in the Middle East? Former Israel Defense Forces head of military intelligence Amos Yadlin, Pulitzer Prize–winning political commentator Charles Krauthammer, CNN host Fareed Zakaria, and Iranian-born academic Vali Nasr debate the consequences of a nuclear-armed Iran.

"Deterring Iran is fundamentally different from deterring the Soviet Union. You could rely on the latter but not the former."
— Charles Krauthammer

www.houseofanansi.com/munkdebates

North America's Lost Decade?

Krugman and Rosenberg vs. Summers and Bremmer

The future of the North American economy is more uncertain than ever. In this edition of the Munk Debates, Nobel Prize–winning economist Paul Krugman and chief economist and strategist at Gluskin Sheff + Associates David Rosenberg square off against former U.S. Treasury secretary Lawrence Summers and bestselling author Ian Bremmer to tackle the resolution: Be it resolved North America faces a Japan-style era of high unemployment and slow growth.

"It's now impossible to deny the obvious, which is that we are not now, and have never been, on the road to recovery."
— Paul Krugman

Does the 21st Century Belong to China?

Kissinger and Zakaria vs. Ferguson and Li

Is China's rise unstoppable? Former U.S. Secretary of State Henry Kissinger and CNN's Fareed Zakaria pair off against leading historian Niall Ferguson and world-renowned Chinese economist David Daokui Li to debate China's emergence as a global force, the key geopolitical issue of our time.

This edition of the Munk Debates also features the first formal public debate Dr. Kissinger has participated in on China's future.

"I have enormous difficulty imagining a world dominated by China . . . I believe the concept that any one country will dominate the world is, in itself, a misunderstanding of the world in which we live now."

— Henry Kissinger

www.houseofanansi.com/munkdebates

Hitchens vs. Blair

Christopher Hitchens vs. Tony Blair

Intellectual juggernaut and staunch atheist Christopher Hitchens goes head-to-head with former British prime minister Tony Blair, one of the Western world's most openly devout political leaders, on the age-old question: Is religion a force for good in the world? Few world leaders have had a greater hand in shaping current events than Blair; few writers have been more outspoken and polarizing than Hitchens.

Sharp, provocative, and thoroughly engrossing, *Hitchens vs. Blair* is a rigorous and electrifying intellectual sparring match on the contentious questions that continue to dog the topic of religion in our globalized world.

"If religious instruction were not allowed until the child had attained the age of reason, we would be living in a very different world."

— Christopher Hitchens

www.houseofanansi.com/munkdebates

The Munk Debates: Volume One

Edited by Rudyard Griffiths; Introduction by Peter Munk

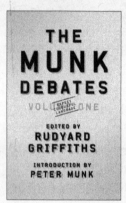

Launched in 2008 by philanthropists Peter and Melanie Munk, the Munk Debates is Canada's premier international debate series, a highly anticipated cultural event that brings together the world's brightest minds.

This volume includes the first five debates in the series, and features twenty leading thinkers and doers arguing for or against provocative resolutions that address pressing public policy concerns, such as the future of global security, the implications of humanitarian intervention, the effectiveness of foreign aid, the threat of climate change, and the state of health care in Canada and the United States.

"By trying to highlight the most important issues at crucial moments in the global conversation, these debates not only profile the ideas and solutions of some of our brightest thinkers and doers, but crystallize public passion and knowledge, helping to tackle some global challenges confronting humankind."

— Peter Munk

www.houseofanansi.com/munkdebates